P9-AEX-778

Retirement and the Hidden Epidemic

RETIREMENT AND THE HIDDEN EPIDEMIC

The Complex Link Between Aging,
Work Disengagement, and Substance
Misuse—and What To Do About It

Peter A. Bamberger

Samuel B. Bacharach

With the assistance of

Kathleen A. Briggs and Meira Ben-Gad

OXFORD
UNIVERSITY PRESS

OXFORD
UNIVERSITY PRESS

Oxford University Press is a department of the University of
Oxford. It furthers the University's objective of excellence in research,
scholarship, and education by publishing worldwide.

Oxford   New York
Auckland   Cape Town   Dar es Salaam   Hong Kong   Karachi
Kuala Lumpur   Madrid   Melbourne   Mexico City   Nairobi
New Delhi   Shanghai   Taipei   Toronto

With offices in
Argentina   Austria   Brazil   Chile   Czech Republic   France   Greece
Guatemala   Hungary   Italy   Japan   Poland   Portugal   Singapore
South Korea   Switzerland   Thailand   Turkey   Ukraine   Vietnam

Oxford is a registered trademark of Oxford University Press
in the UK and certain other countries.

Published in the United States of America by
Oxford University Press
198 Madison Avenue, New York, NY 10016

Library of Congress Cataloging-in-Publication Data
Bamberger, Peter.
Retirement and the hidden epidemic : the complex link between aging,
work disengagement, and substance misuse—and what to do about it /
by Peter A. Bamberger, Samuel B. Bacharach.
    pages cm
Includes bibliographical references and index.
ISBN 978–0–19–937412–0
1. Retirees—Alcohol use—United States.   2. Retirees—Substance abuse—
United States.   3. Retirees—United States—Psychology.   4. Alcoholism—
United States.   5. Aging—United States—Psychological aspects.
I. Bacharach, Samuel B.   II. Title.
HV5138.B36 2014
362.29084'60973—dc23
2013044579

9 8 7 6 5 4 3 2
Printed in the United States of America
on acid-free paper

In memory of R. Brinkley Smithers

In celebration of Adele Smithers

ACKNOWLEDGEMENTS

The authors wish to express gratitude for the years of support from R. Brinkley Smithers and Adele Smithers. The Smithers' tradition of leading the battle against the disease of alcoholism has inspired our work for the last 20 years. Their support of the R. Brinkley Smithers Institute for Alcohol-Related Workplace Studies at Cornell University has made all our work possible. We also would like to acknowledge the support we received from the National Institute on Alcoholism and Alcohol Abuse (NIAAA), the sponsor of our 10-year study on retirement and alcohol use (R01 AA011976). With special gratitude to Marcia Scott of NIAAA who served as a guide throughout this research project. Stacia Murphy, past president of the National Council on Alcoholism and Drug Dependence (NCADD) has always been a strong supporter of our research agenda. A special thanks to Yasamin Miller and her colleagues at Cornell's Survey Research Institute, for being great partners in data collection. Our gratitude to Dean Harry Katz and his support of the mission of the Smithers Institute. Lastly, we wish to thank our colleagues, William J. Sonnenstuhl and Kathleen Briggs, who have been supportive of all our research efforts.

CONTENTS

LIST OF ABBREVIATIONS

AA	Alcoholics Anonymous
AUDIT	Alcohol Use Disorders Identification Test
BRITE	Brief Intervention and Treatment for Elders
CAGE	Cut down, Annoyed, Guilty, Eye-opener (substance use screening test)
CBT	Cognitive behavioral therapy
CDC	Centers for Disease Control and Prevention
DAST	Drug Abuse Screening Test
DAWN	Drug Abuse Warning Network
DB	Defined benefit (pension plan)
DC	Defined contribution (pension plan)
DPI	Drinking Problems Index
DSM-IV	Diagnostic and Statistical Manual of Mental Disorders, fourth edition
EAP	Employee assistance program
GOAL	Guiding Older Adult Lifestyles
HPA	Hypothalamic–pituitary–adrenal
MAST	Michigan Alcohol Screening Test
NSDUH	National Survey on Drug Use and Health
PAP	Peer assistance program
P–E Fit	Person–environment fit
SAMHSA	Substance Abuse and Mental Health Services Administration
TrEAT	Trial for Early Alcohol Treatment

Retirement and the Hidden Epidemic

CHAPTER 1

Retirement and Alcohol: The Magnitude of the Problem

On January 1, 2011, the first Baby Boomers celebrated their 65th birthdays. Since then, members of the Boomer generation have crossed that threshold at the rate of some 10,000 per day, and they will continue to do so until 2030, when, according to the Pew Research Center, the proportion of the US population aged 65 and up will have reached at least 18% (Cohn & Taylor, 2010). This trend is both reflective of and a contributing factor behind the rapid aging of the US population, a consequence of lower birth rates combined with higher life expectancies (Wang & Shultz, 2010). Life expectancy at birth in the United States was about 70 years in 1960, 74 in 1980, 77 in 2000, and 78 in 2009 (Arias, 2011; Kochanek, Xu, Murphy, Miniño, & Kung, 2011). Someone who turned 50 in 1960 could expect to live about 25 more years; in 2007, the average 50-year-old could expect another 31 years of life (Arias, 2011). And these trends are only likely to accelerate as medical advances continue to make headway against diseases that affect older people (heart disease, cancer).

With more people living longer, alcohol-related problems among older segments of the population have drawn increasing attention from medical and public health professionals (Gallo, 2012; Kuerbis & Sacco, 2012). These problems are often manifested in at-risk and problem drinking. *At-risk drinking* means drinking more than recommended limits; *problem drinking* means continued drinking despite an adverse effect on the drinker's physical or mental health, social interactions, or daily functioning. Evidence from both local and national surveys suggests that at-risk and problem drinking among older adults in the United States is a major hidden health threat, with broad implications for the welfare and quality of life of older drinkers and their families. Conservative estimates put the rate of problem drinking among adults aged 65 and over at around 10% (Blazer & Wu, 2009a; Moos, Schutte, Brennan, & Moos, 2009). Other analyses suggest that the numbers may be even higher; for instance, Blow (1998) found that problem drinking may affect up to 17% of all adults aged 60 and above and more than 21% of men over 49. (All figures given apply to the United States.) The prevalence of alcohol-related problems seems to be particularly high in health care settings, reaching around 20% for older patients in emergency rooms (Kuerbis & Sacco, 2012), nursing homes (Kennedy, Efremova, Frazier, & Saba, 1999), and psychiatric wards (National Institute on Alcohol Abuse and Alcoholism, 1998).

Disturbingly, even higher estimates of problem or at-risk drinking in older populations may underestimate the true extent of the problem. Comparing studies is difficult in general, both because older adults are not regularly screened for alcohol misuse or for drinking problems and because the few studies directed at this question vary in the populations they focus on, the questions they ask, and the instruments they use (Merrick et al., 2008). But there are several ways in which surveys may underestimate the prevalence of unhealthy drinking in older populations. First, questionnaires used to screen for at-risk or problem drinking may not sufficiently tap the adverse consequences of drinking for older adults, who may not experience the social and occupational ramifications of alcohol misuse often used to diagnose drinking problems (National Institute on Alcohol Abuse and Alcoholism, 1998). Older people—along with their family members and care professionals—may also mistake symptoms of alcohol-related problems, such as depression, confusion, or frequent falls, for medical or psychiatric conditions common in the elderly (Kennedy et al., 1999; National Institute on Alcohol Abuse and Alcoholism, 1998). When answering questions about the quantity or frequency of their drinking, older individuals may underreport their own alcohol use, either inadvertently, due to memory problems or difficulty with computation, or deliberately, because of the stigma they feel is attached to drinking (Dufour & Fuller, 1995). Finally, population studies are subject to additional sources of error, in that they may fail to capture individuals in health care settings, where older people with drinking problems are likely to be overrepresented (Dufour & Fuller, 1995), and in that excess mortality among heavy drinkers may leave a surviving population that consumes less alcohol (National Institute on Alcohol Abuse and Alcoholism, 1998). Table 1.1 summarizes these potential problems.

Table 1.1. WHY SURVEYS MIGHT UNDERESTIMATE THE PREVALENCE OF AT-RISK OR PROBLEM DRINKING AMONG OLDER ADULTS

Older adults are not regularly screened for alcohol problems.

Tools commonly used to screen for alcohol problems may not be applicable to older adults.

Effects of alcohol problems (e.g., depression, confusion, falls) may be mistaken for normal signs of aging.

Older people may underreport their drinking deliberately (out of guilt or shame).

Older people may underreport their drinking inadvertently (due to memory problems or difficulty with computation).

Population studies may fail to capture individuals in health care settings.

Excess mortality among heavy drinkers may leave a surviving population that consumes less alcohol.

Of equal concern is the possibility that the number of older adults with drinking problems is likely to rise over the coming years, not only because of the aging of the population but also because of shifting societal and cultural norms. While by most accounts people tend to drink less as they grow older (e.g., Brennan & Moos, 1990; Grant et al., 2004), there is evidence that individuals follow relatively stable drinking patterns as they age (National Institute on Alcohol Abuse and Alcoholism, 1998). If that is the case, the Boomer generation may show a higher prevalence of problems with alcohol as they enter later life than previous generations, who came of age at times when alcohol use was less socially accepted (the same is true for illicit drugs; Reardon, 2012). Moreover, some research suggests that the prevalence and severity of problem drinking may in fact increase as a function of age in older populations, especially among individuals with a history of drinking problems (Atkinson, Tolson, & Turner, 1990; Brennan, Schutte, & Moos, 1999; National Institute on Alcohol Abuse and Alcoholism, 2000).

If indeed people's drinking trajectories over time tend to be established in part by societal norms that prevailed when they were young, current trends should be a source of serious concern. The picture presented by Moos et al. (2009) is instructive. Moos and his colleagues tracked 719 nonabstaining adults in one community sample over 20 years, beginning when the participants were 55 to 65 years old. At the start of the study, 65% of the men and 49% of the women reported consuming more than recommended guidelines of seven drinks per week or two drinks in any one day at least once over the previous month. When the participants were 75 to 85 years old, these figures had declined somewhat but were still relatively high, at 49% of the men and 27% of the women. Moreover, 32% of the men and 12% of the women reported drinking at even higher thresholds—more than 14 drinks per week or three drinks in any one day. Of course, as Moos et al. point out, their sample is not representative of the entire population, in terms of both demographics (all participants were drawn from one geographic region) and drinking patterns (the sample excluded abstainers). But their findings show that many older adults who drink fail to adhere to recommended limits for alcohol consumption, even into their eighth and ninth decades.

A WORD TO THE WISE: KEY TERMS

Before we continue, a few definitions are in order. The lay and scholarly literatures offer various ways to speak about alcohol use, misuse, and abuse, including at-risk drinking, unhealthy drinking, heavy drinking, binge drinking, problem drinking, alcoholism, alcohol dependence, and alcohol use disorders. Some of these terms are used differently by different authors, and some overlap in meaning. The following will serve as a general guide.

In general, *at-risk drinking, unhealthy drinking,* and *heavy drinking* all denote drinking more than recommended guidelines, such as those of the National Institute on Alcohol Abuse and Alcoholism or the American Geriatrics Society. A number of guidelines for adults aged 65 and above can be found in the literature, but one that is widely accepted (including by both the American Geriatrics Society and the National Institute on Alcohol Abuse and Alcoholism) is a maximum of seven drinks per week or two drinks on any one occasion, where a drink is defined as a 4- or 5-ounce glass of wine, a 12-ounce can of beer, or a 1- or 1.5-ounce shot of distilled spirits (each of these drinks contains about 0.6 fluid ounces of ethanol). Such guidelines offer a likely upper limit of the amount of alcohol that can be consumed before the drinker risks suffering adverse consequences. Note, though, that guidelines are general by nature and do not take account of individual differences—for example, in health or body weight—that might affect any given drinker's actual risk. Some published guidelines differ for men and women, with women's limits being slightly lower. But many clinicians believe that older adult men and women should limit themselves to the same relatively low levels of alcohol use.

Binge drinking refers to periodic heavy drinking. Binge drinking may be defined differently by different authors, with varying criteria depending on the general age of the population under investigation. For older adults in general, binge drinking means drinking four or more (for men) or three or more (for women) drinks in any drinking episode (Kuerbis & Sacco, 2012).

Problem drinking denotes drinking despite adverse medical, psychological, or social consequences (Barry, Oslin, & Blow, 2001). That is, it means continued drinking even in the presence of effects on the drinker's physical health, mental health, social interactions, or daily functioning. It is important to emphasize that problem drinking is defined by its consequences rather than by the amount or frequency of alcohol consumed. A person may have drinking problems even if his or her consumption falls below formal guidelines (Barry et al., 2001).

Alcohol misuse can be used to mean at-risk drinking generally or any incident of binge drinking or drinking to the point of drunkenness. It is to be distinguished from *alcohol abuse* and *alcohol dependence*, which are diagnostic terms used by the American Psychiatric Association. Essentially, alcohol abuse involves episodic but recurrent misuse that threatens the individual's health and well-being, interpersonal relationships, or ability to meet commitments and responsibilities. Alcohol dependence symptoms fall into four categories: a craving for alcohol, impaired control (difficulty limiting the amount drunk on any given occasion), physical dependence (marked by withdrawal symptoms, such as sweating or nausea, when alcohol use is stopped), and physical tolerance (the need for increasing amounts of alcohol in order to feel its effects) (Barrick & Connors, 2002). Alcohol abuse and dependence are known popularly as *alcoholism*.

The distinction between *abuse* and *dependence* is widely agreed to be of minimal value when dealing with some populations, including older people (Kennedy et al., 1999). For this reason, the American Psychiatric Association has introduced the term *alcohol use disorder* to encompass the diagnostic criteria for alcohol abuse and alcohol dependence (see Tables 1.2 and 1.3).

Table 1.2. KEY TERMS

At-risk, unhealthy, or heavy drinking	Drinking beyond recommended daily or weekly guidelines. A widely accepted guideline for adults over 65 is a maximum of seven drinks per week or two drinks in any one day, where a drink is defined as a 5-ounce glass of wine, a 12-ounce can of beer, or a 1.5-ounce shot of distilled spirits (e.g., gin or vodka).
Periodic heavy drinking ("binge drinking")	For adults over the age of 65, commonly defined as drinking four or more (men) or three or more (women) drinks at any one time.
Problem drinking	Continued drinking despite adverse consequences to the individual's physical health, mental health, social interactions, or daily functioning.
Alcohol use disorders	Used by the American Psychiatric Association to encompass both alcohol abuse and alcohol dependence (see Table 1.3).
Alcoholism	The popular term for alcohol use disorders.

Table 1.3. ALCOHOL USE DISORDER

Diagnostic Criteria

A problematic pattern of alcohol use leading to clinically significant impairment or distress, as manifested by at least two of the following, occurring within a 12-month period:

- Alcohol is often taken in larger amounts or over a longer period than was intended.
- There is a persistent desire or unsuccessful efforts to cut down or control alcohol use.
- A great deal of time is spent in activities necessary to obtain alcohol, use alcohol, or recover from its effects.
- Craving, or a strong desire or urge to use alcohol.
- Recurrent alcohol use resulting in a failure to fulfill major role obligations at work, school, or home.
- Continued alcohol use despite having persistent or recurrent social or interpersonal problems caused or exacerbated by the effects of alcohol.
- Important social, occupational, or recreational activities are given up or reduced because of alcohol use.
- Recurrent alcohol use in situations in which it is physically hazardous.
- Alcohol use is continued despite knowledge of having a persistent or recurrent physical or psychological problem that is likely to have been caused or exacerbated by alcohol.
- Tolerance, as defined by either of the following:
  - A need for markedly increased amounts of alcohol to achieve intoxication or desired effect.
  - A markedly diminished effect with continued use of the same amount of alcohol.
- Withdrawal, as manifested by either of the following:
  - The characteristic withdrawal syndrome for alcohol (refer to Criteria A and B of the criteria set for alcohol withdrawal).
  - Alcohol (or a closely related substance, such as a benzodiazepine) is taken to relieve or avoid withdrawal symptoms.

Note. From American Psychiatric Association. (2013). *Diagnostic and Statistical Manual of Mental Disorders* (5th ed.) Washington, DC: Author. Copyright 2013 by APA. Reprinted with permission.

A number of questionnaires have been developed to screen for drinking problems in various age groups (see Cherpitel, 1997, and Connors & Volk, 2004, for reviews). One instrument specifically designed for use with older people is the Drinking Problems Index, or DPI (Finney, Moos, & Brennan, 1991). Respondents are asked how often over the last 12 months they experienced various events on a 5-point scale (1 = never, 2 = once or twice, 3 = occasionally, 4 = fairly often, and 5 = often). The 17 items of the DPI are shown in Table 1.4. (The DPI and other screening tools will be discussed further in chapter 7.)

Table 1.4. DRINKING PROBLEMS INDEX

In the last 12 months, how often have you:

a. Become "high" after drinking

b. Had a fall or accident as a result of drinking

c. Felt confused after drinking

d. Had a friend worry or complain about your drinking

e. Neglected your appearance because of drinking

f. Had problems occur between you and a member of your family because of your drinking

g. Gone to anyone for help about your drinking

h. Neglected your work because of drinking

i. Lost friends because of your drinking

j. Become intoxicated or drunk after drinking

k. Skipped meals because of drinking

l. Had a family member worry or complain about your drinking

m. Felt you were spending too much money on drinking

n. Felt isolated from people because of your drinking

o. Had a drink to help you forget your worries

p. Had a craving for a drink the first thing after you woke up

q. Neglected the appearance of your living quarters because of drinking

To score the DPI, we count the number of affirmative responses to individual items. Specifically, we first recode the response scale from 0 (never) to 4 (often). Next, we assign one point to each item whose value ranges from 1 to 4. However, because becoming high and drinking to forget are mild drinking problem criteria, we assign one point to these items (*a* and *o*) only if they have a value of 3 or 4. We then sum the points over the items.

Note. From Finney, J. W., Moos, R. H., & Brennan, P. L. (1991). The Drinking Problems Index: A measure to assess alcohol-related problems among older adults. *Journal of Substance Abuse, 3,* 395–404. Copyright 1986 by Rudolf H. Moos, Department of Psychiatry and Behavioral Sciences, Stanford University Medical Center, Palo Alto, CA 94305. Reprinted with permission.

ALCOHOL AND THE PHYSIOLOGY OF AGING

Why are limits on alcohol use so important? Can't older adults be allowed to relax with a few drinks? Haven't they earned the right to enjoy themselves?

Whatever terminology one uses, experts agree that even relatively small quantities of alcohol can have a significant impact on the health and functioning of older adults—much more so than the same amount of alcohol would affect younger people. Research suggests that as people age, they become more sensitive to the physiological effects of alcohol, for several reasons. Most importantly, aging is accompanied by a decrease in lean body mass (that portion of the body's mass not comprising fat, i.e., organs, blood, bones, and muscle). This reduction in lean body mass brings a corresponding shrinkage in the volume of total body water, meaning that there is less fluid available to dilute any alcohol consumed. The result is that the same amount of alcohol will produce a higher blood alcohol concentration in older adults compared with younger ones (Dufour & Fuller, 1995; Oslin, 2000; Smith, 1995). Aging may also diminish the body's ability to metabolize alcohol (Kennedy et al., 1999; Merrick et al., 2008), meaning that any alcohol consumed remains longer in the blood, whence it is distributed to the brain and other tissues. Finally, there is also evidence that aging increases the permeability of the blood–brain barrier and increases the sensitivity of receptors that alcohol binds to in the brain (Kennedy et al., 1999). Both of these processes have the effect of intensifying the effects of alcohol on the brain. All this is in addition to the fact that the natural effects of aging on the body's cellular repair processes mean that the older body is less able to repair alcohol-related damage to cells and tissues, whether in the brain or other organs (Oslin, 2000).

Falls and injuries are a particular area of concern in older people who drink as the effects of alcohol can exacerbate age-related changes in the body's ability to regulate posture and balance (National Institute on Alcohol Abuse and Alcoholism, 1998). The basic activities of daily life can become extra hazardous when alcohol is involved; in one national sample of men 50 years and older, Perreira and Sloan (2002) found that heavy periodic drinking quadrupled individuals' risk of developing functional impairments in their ability to perform such daily activities as getting out of bed, crossing a room, and dressing. A history of problem drinking has also been found to increase the onset of major depression and other psychiatric problems, as well as memory loss (National Institute on Alcohol Abuse and Alcoholism, 1998; Perreira & Sloan, 2002). The logic behind these associations is not difficult to discern. Aging and alcohol misuse both cause a loss of tissue in crucial areas of the brain, including the frontal lobes (key to cognitive functioning and memory) and the cerebellum (which helps regulate balance and posture). Magnetic resonance imaging has revealed more brain tissue loss in older adults with alcohol abuse disorders than in either younger alcoholics or older adults who were not alcoholics (National Institute on Alcohol Abuse and Alcoholism, 1998). Alcoholism also seems to heighten the decrease in bone density that accompanies aging, putting those who fall at greater risk for debilitating hip fractures (National Institute on Alcohol Abuse and Alcoholism, 1998).

Two related characteristics of older adults also contribute to putting people in this age group at greater risk from alcohol consumption. The first is the high prevalence of chronic health conditions among older people.

Many of the conditions for which older people seek health care—including hypertension, diabetes, depression, dementia, liver disease, cardiovascular disease, and sleep disturbances—can be influenced by drinking (Adams, 2002; Kennedy et al., 1999; Oslin, 2000). The American Geriatrics Society (2008) includes ulcers, gastrointestinal bleeding, gout, anxiety, and gait disorders among the chronic conditions that can be triggered or worsened by alcohol. Drinking too much can raise the level of some fats in the blood and increase blood pressure—both factors that contribute to heart disease (National Institute on Alcohol Abuse and Alcoholism, 1998).

The second characteristic that heightens the risk of alcohol consumption in older people is their high use of both prescription and over-the-counter medications. Both acute and chronic alcohol intake can lead to interactions with various drugs often found in the pharmacopoeias of older people. For instance, acute intake (i.e., drinking more than some minimum amount at any given time) can increase the sedative effects of psychotropic drugs (Adams, 2002; Kennedy et al., 1999); these include medications prescribed for mood disorders, to slow the progression of Alzheimer disease, or as sleep aids. Alcohol can trigger so-called disulfiram-like reactions (including shortness of breath, rapid heart rate, nausea, vomiting, headache, confusion, fainting, and circulatory collapse) when consumed in combination with certain medications, including cephalosporins (a type of antibiotic) and drugs used in the treatment of diabetes (sulfonylurea and hypoglycemics). Acute alcohol intake can temporarily increase the effects of anticoagulants, hypoglycemics, and phenytoin (an antiseizure medication). Meanwhile, chronic use of alcohol activates enzymes that break down toxins, including alcohol; these enzymes may also break down prescription medications, reducing their effectiveness (Kennedy et al., 1999; National Institute on Alcohol Abuse and Alcoholism, 1998). Some common drug–alcohol interactions are shown in Table 1.5.

The American Geriatrics Society (2008) suggests that alcohol may interact inversely, in one way or another, with all available prescription and nonprescription medications, meaning that any older person who takes so much as indigestion tablets (H_2 blockers) on a regular basis may be affected. Moreover, because medical personnel and caregivers may expect the elderly to be confused or disoriented or to have slow reflexes, they may mistake the signs of alcohol–drug interactions for "normal" signs of aging or as symptoms of disorders such as dementia. The result can be a worsening spiral of medication and further degeneration or, at the very least, missed opportunities to improve the older person's quality of life by diagnosing unhealthy drinking.

Table 1.5. SOME COMMON MEDICATIONS THAT MAY INTERACT INVERSELY WITH ALCOHOL

Alcohol combined with...	... may cause the following:
H₂ blockers, aspirin	May raise alcohol levels.
Benzodiazepines, tricyclic antidepressants, narcotics, barbiturates, antihistamines	May increase sedation and impair psychomotor function.
Aspirin, NSAIDs	May increase bleeding time and cause gastric inflammation and bleeding.
Metronidazole, sulfonamides, longer-acting oral hypoglycemics (tolbutamide, chlorpropamide)	May cause disulfiram-like response, with nausea and vomiting.
Reserpine, aldomet, nitroglycerin, hydralazine	May produce hypotension.
Acetaminophen, isoniazid, phenylbutazone	May increase hepatotoxicity.
Antihypertensives, antidiabetic drugs, drugs for ulcers, gout, and heart failure	May exacerbate the underlying disease.
Benzodiazepines, narcotics, barbiturates, warfarin, propranolol, isoniazid, tolbutamide	May alter drug metabolism.

Note. Adapted from American Geriatrics Society. (2008, September 5). Alcohol use disorders in older adults. *Annals of Long-Term Care: Clinical Care and Aging.* Retrieved from http://www.annalsoflong-termcare.com/article/5143. NSAID = nonsteroidal anti-inflammatory drug.

There is some evidence that moderate alcohol use can have beneficial effects in otherwise healthy older adults (Oslin, 2000). Studies of the general population suggest that one or two standard drinks per day for men and one for women may offer some protection against heart disease (American Heart Association, 2011). Although research on this question in older people is limited, there is evidence that moderate drinking also has a protective effect among those older than 65. However, this area of investigation is still fairly new, and it is unclear to what degree the benefits of moderate alcohol intake continue as people get older—or to what degree those possible benefits may be offset by the potential negative effects. For instance, Oslin (2000) points out that consuming more than seven drinks per week may decrease the risk of strokes caused by blocked blood vessels but may increase the risk of strokes caused by bleeding.

Given the implications of alcohol misuse on the physical and emotional well-being of people in late life, it is unsurprising that alcohol misuse features strongly among older adults in health care settings. Kuerbis and Sacco (2012) cite research suggesting that the prevalence of alcohol use disorders may be as high as 22% of older people who are medical inpatients or who present to the emergency room. Kennedy et al. (1999) found that 20% of nursing home patients have a history of alcohol abuse or dependence. According to the National Institute on Alcohol Abuse and Alcoholism

(1998), surveys suggest that 6% to 11% of elderly patients admitted to hospitals exhibit symptoms of alcoholism, as do 14% of those seen in emergency rooms and 20% of those in psychiatric wards. Alcohol-related health problems account for more than $60 billion a year in hospital-related costs (Schonfeld & Dupree, 1995). And with the graying of the population, these figures are likely to rise dramatically. By the end of the first quarter of the 21st century, the number of older people in the health care system with alcohol-related problems is expected to be nearly double the number at the century's start (Gfroerer, Penne, Pemberton, & Folsom, 2003).

WHO IS AT RISK?

In contemporary Western society, alcohol has various cultural connotations. There's the hard-drinking, hail-fellow-well-met type and the lonely old alcoholic, as well as the beer culture of the working man and the cocktail parties of the upper class. As could be expected, research suggests that each of these stereotypes tells something of the truth but not the whole truth.

It is clear that not all older people are equally predisposed to fall prey to unhealthy or problem drinking. Studies have identified various attributes, including both sociodemographic factors and individual traits, that are associated with greater at-risk drinking in later life (Kuerbis & Sacco, 2012). These include gender, age, race or ethnicity, education, income, physical and mental health, coping style, previous use of alcohol or other substances, and experiencing various life events such as divorce.

Demographic Factors

Over all age groups, men are more likely than women to drink and are likely to drink in larger amounts (e.g., Centers for Disease Control and Prevention, 2012; Nolen-Hoeksema, 2004). It is therefore not surprising that studies consistently find that older men have a higher prevalence of unhealthy drinking than older women. Two examples from among many will suffice. Merrick et al. (2008) analyzed data from a national survey of community-dwelling Medicare beneficiaries aged 65 and above on two parameters: drinking more than recommended guidelines (defined as 30 drinks per month) or heavy episodic drinking (four or more drinks in a single day). A full 16% of the men but only 4% of the women in their sample reported engaging in unhealthy drinking based on one or both parameters. Meanwhile, Breslow, Faden, and Smothers (2003) estimated the prevalence of alcohol consumption in Americans aged 65 and older using data from three nationally representative cross-sectional surveys: the National Health Interview Survey of 2000, the Behavioral Risk Factor Surveillance System of 2001, and the National Household Survey on Drug Abuse of 2000.[1] They found that, for men, rates of moderate drinking as measured by the three surveys (no more than one drink per day) ranged from about 27% to about 39% and rates of heavier drinking ranged around 9% or 10%. In women, rates of moderate drinking were about 21% to 32% and rates of heavier drinking were 2% to 3%.

Almost all studies of drinking in older people, including those that track individuals over time as well as those that compare different age cohorts at one time point, have found that the "young old"—that is, people in their 60s and early 70s—tend to drink more than those in their late 70s and beyond. To cite Merrick et al. (2008) again, in that study respondents aged 81 and above were most likely to be nondrinkers and least likely to report unhealthy drinking (4.9% versus 13% for those aged 65–70). Similar results were found by Moore et al. (2009), Moos et al. (2009), and many others. But, as we noted above, surveys of drinking among the very old may be misleading as older people who drink more may be less likely to live into their 80s and 90s. Other factors, such as gender, may also interact with age to influence drinking patterns. For instance, Breslow et al. (2003) found that in increasingly older groups of men moderate drinking remained stable while heavier drinking decreased (in two of the three surveys analyzed), while for women the pattern was the opposite: Moderate drinking decreased in increasingly older groups of women, but heavier drinking remained stable.

In general, studies that have examined relationships between demographic factors and drinking have painted a fairly consistent picture of the older drinker. Besides the findings we have already discussed regarding age and gender, alcohol use tends to be higher among people who are white, divorced or separated, less religious, in generally good health, and highly educated and who possess greater financial resources (Kuerbis & Sacco, 2012; Merrick et al., 2008; Moore et al., 2009; Platt, Sloan, & Costanzo, 2010). Some of these factors will be discussed further below.

Physical and Mental Health

The relationship between health and drinking is complex and involves multiple chains of causation and relationship. Evidence suggests that, overall, older people who are in better health are more likely to drink and are likely to drink more than their age-mates in poorer health (Kuerbis & Sacco,

2012; Merrick et al., 2008; Moore et al., 2009). At the same time, people who drink heavily in late life typically report poorer physical and mental health than those who restrict their consumption (Kuerbis & Sacco, 2012). Moos, Brennan, Schutte, and Moos (2010), to cite one example, found that, in general, health-related problems increased and alcohol consumption declined over the 20 years of their study as their sample matured from age 55–65 to 75–85 years. Also, acute health events were associated with less alcohol consumption. However, a significant subset of individuals with greater health burdens relied on alcohol to reduce pain.

Coping Style

Studies have found that how individuals tend to cope with stress is a good predictor of whether or not they are likely to have a drinking problem in late life (Kuerbis & Sacco, 2012). For instance, Platt et al. (2010) found that individuals who relied on avoidance coping were more likely to develop and maintain alcohol-related problems as they aged. This finding makes intuitive sense, given alcohol's ready availability as a means of self-medicating psychological tension as well as physical pain (Conger, 1956).

Unsurprisingly, too, people who have a history of relying on substances to reduce tension have been found to be at greater risk for at-risk drinking and drinking problems in later life (Moos, Schutte, Brennan, & Moos, 2010). A history of drinking problems by middle age is a very strong predictor of late-life drinking problems (Platt et al., 2010; Moos, Brennan, et al., 2010).

Life Events

Research suggests that various life events can precipitate increased drinking. Both Merrick et al. (2008) and Moore et al. (2009) found that older people who were divorced, separated, or single were more likely to drink and to drink at unhealthy levels than married people. However, Moore et al. (2009) found that married respondents were more likely to drink than those who were widowed. In Perreira and Sloan's (2001) 6-year panel study of people in their 50s and 60s, widowhood was associated with increased drinking but only for a short time. These findings are in keeping with evidence that drinking has a strong social component (Adams, 1996; Kuerbis & Sacco, 2012; Oslin, 2000), one which may decline in importance after a spouse passes away.

Retirement is another life event that looms large as a potential source of influence on drinking patterns. Yet as we shall see in this book, the link between retirement and alcohol use is not straightforward.

RETIREMENT AS A PERIOD OF TRANSITION

Before we go any further, we'd like to highlight the following caveat: The literature on retirement and drinking behavior that we will discuss in the following chapters is, by necessity, incomplete, a function of the rapidly changing nature of retirement.

Among the many social and economic shifts associated with the aging of the population in Western countries, one that stands out is a change in how we perceive and experience retirement. Not too long ago, retirement was almost always a discrete event, a clear demarcation between work (before) and nonwork (after). Today retirement is more often experienced as a process, in which "retirees" move in and out of the labor force, working full- or part-time, changing careers or starting their own business, along with more traditional retirement activities like volunteering or helping their grown children with child care (Shultz & Wang, 2011; Wang, 2007; Wang & Shultz, 2010). Movement back into the labor force following retirement from a career job is known as "bridge employment," and it is increasingly widespread. Cahill, Giandrea, and Quinn (2006; see also Cahill, Giandrea, & Quinn, 2007) estimate that 6 of every 10 Americans who are still in full-time career jobs after age 50 take a bridge job following retirement. In a recent survey of employed individuals aged 45 and older, AARP (formerly the American Association of Retired Persons) found that 69% either held bridge jobs or planned to be in bridge employment during retirement (Brown, 2003). In Canada, Hébert and Luong (2008), using data covering 97% of the population, calculated that the proportion of individuals aged 50 to 69 who were in bridge employment rose from 7.9% in 1999 to 9.7% in 2004. A full 18% of the Canadian population then aged 65 to 69 were in bridge employment in 2004.

These changes to the retirement landscape have been influenced by a number of factors. Financial considerations are one. The economic stresses associated with the new demographics mean that retirement benefits and savings may not provide the stable income their owners expected. Meanwhile, private employers are responding to uncertain economic conditions by amending their benefits packages, shifting some of the risk in pension schemes to employees and eliminating health care benefits for retirees (Wang & Shultz, 2010). Cahill et al. (2006, 2007) identified the shift from defined-benefit (DB) to defined-contribution (DC) pension plans, such as 401(k)s, as a significant driver of changes in workers' retirement decisions. They found that individuals with either no pension plan or a DC pension plan were more likely to take on bridge jobs (66% of men and 67% of women with no pension plan, 59% of men and 53% of women with DC pensions) than those with DB pensions (46% of men and 50% of women with such plans). These gaps are only likely to widen with current trends. Cahill et al. point out that between 1983 and 2004 the proportion of US private-sector employees with pension coverage who had only a DB plan declined from over 60% to 20%, while the proportion with only a DC plan snowballed from 12% to more than 60%. As their data precede the widespread recession that began in 2007 and 2008, the shifts from DB to DC have likely increased.

Another factor is that with the better health care and longer life expectancies we now enjoy, people who are old enough to retire often don't actually feel old. In the Pew Research Center's recent survey of attitudes among the Boomer generation (Cohn & Taylor, 2010), 61% of respondents said they felt younger than their chronological age—typically, a full 9 years younger. A 65-year-old who feels 56 or a 70-year-old who feels 61 may not be prepared to punch the clock or lock the office door for the last time. Indeed, the AARP survey (Brown, 2003) found that a large number of working retirees were employed mainly for noneconomic reasons (e.g., to remain active or stay useful).

Cahill et al. (2006, 2007) captured the two sets of factors fueling the decline in traditional retirement with their finding that the prevalence of bridge employment was highest among those with either high or low socio-economic status, with both low-wage, low-skilled workers and high-wage, high-skilled workers more likely to take bridge jobs after retirement than those in the middle. They argue that "these relationships highlight the difference between those who chose bridge jobs voluntarily (those who want to work) and those who did so out of financial necessity (those who have to work)" (Cahill et al., 2007, p. 6).

On the basis of their own and others' findings, AARP suggested that receiving retirement benefits or living off retirement savings, rather than complete labor-force disengagement, should be viewed as the defining characteristic of retirement (Brown, 2003). Others argue that the concept of retirement is subjective and has more to do with how people define themselves than the number of hours they work or the proportion of income that is derived from savings or benefits (Cahill, Giandrea, & Quinn, 2012). Whatever their specific proposals, though, those with an interest in the subject are in agreement on one thing: The old notion of "retirement" needs to be, well, retired.

RETIREMENT AND ALCOHOL USE: WHY SHOULD EMPLOYERS CARE?

Should employers and organizations be concerned about a possible link between retirement and alcohol use and misuse? After all, one might argue, if "retired" workers are still in the labor force in some form, presumably they are subject to the same influences and pressures as other, non-retired employees. As for those who have disengaged from work entirely, they are no longer the employer's problem. Yet both of these attitudes are shortsighted.

There are as yet almost no data on how the changing retirement landscape, and in particular the rise in bridge employment, might affect the relationship between the transition out of the workforce and alcohol use (other than findings from one of our own studies, which we discuss in chapter 3). But studies on other aspects of bridge employment suggest that this group of workers is not simply a subset of the larger working population. Rather, bridge employees seem to resemble nonretired workers in some respects and retirees in others (Cahill et al., 2012; Zhan, Wang, Liu, & Shultz, 2009). Their retired status thus needs to be taken into account in any consideration of this group's attitudes and behavior.

The arguments that can be adduced for how bridge employment might affect drinking behavior seem to cut both ways. First, some evidence suggests that bridge employment in general lowers health risks. For instance, Zhan et al. (2009) found that retirees who held bridge jobs experienced fewer major diseases and functional limitations than those who had fully disengaged from the workforce, even after controlling for baseline health status. In addition, retirees who took bridge jobs in their career field, as opposed to some other type of work, experienced better mental as well as physical health. Zhan et al. posited that this finding might reflect a propensity for individuals in bridge jobs outside their career field to be there because they need to continue working, not because they want to (p. 385). Such findings suggest that, in theory at least, bridge employment may be risky only if it is characterized by any of the risk factors associated with substance misuse more generally—for example, a stressful or aversive work environment or permissive drinking norms (we will cover these and other risk factors in chapter 2).

On the other hand, there are several reasons why, regardless of the work context, bridge employment by its nature may heighten the risk of substance misuse. For instance, even if they are working in their career field, bridge employees may be new to their jobs and, thus, may face all the sources of stress associated with starting a new job at any age (Kammeyer-Mueller,

Wanberg, Rubenstein, & Song, 2012). In addition, as older adults, bridge employees may bring with them a different set of skills and expectations than younger hires, potentially hampering their integration into the new work environment. Under such conditions, alcohol might serve as a ready means of reducing the tension arising from new workplace demands (cognitive or physical) and age discrimination (real or perceived). Bridge employees may also use drinking to form social bonds with current employees. Finally, many bridge employees work on a part-time basis, making them less exposed to systems of workplace control. That is, with part-timers being "under the radar," it may be more difficult for management or peers to identify a substance misuse problem and intervene.

As noted above, these considerations are all speculative at this stage. Indeed, to reiterate an important point we made earlier in this chapter, the risks of substance abuse are in general lower for older workers than for the emerging adult workforce, simply because of the fall in substance misuse rates with age. However, with many organizations turning to the recently "retired" as a critical workforce, employers should not assume that older people are inherently unlikely to engage in misuse.

What about the argument that retirees who are no longer in the workforce are not of interest to organizations and employers? Our response to this claim is that the health care costs associated with older adults' substance misuse affect all members of society, and employers in particular, by raising the costs of health care and social welfare. In the United States, FICA (the Federal Insurance Contributions Act) requires employers not only to withhold Social Security and Medicare taxes from their employees' wages but also to remit a matching contribution to the federal government. With every increase in the health care costs of older citizens, the pressure on Social Security and Medicare intensifies—and the contributions required from both workers and employers must rise to help meet the growing need.

WHAT TO EXPECT FROM THIS BOOK

Over the past quarter-century or so, the relationship between retirement and alcohol use has been the subject of a small but growing body of research. The bulk of this literature offers, at best, a cloudy picture of this relationship. Yet our knowledge and understanding are becoming sharper over time as investigators gain a deeper sense of the tools and research questions that will offer more fruitful insights.

The present volume offers an up-to-date perspective on the retirement–alcohol relationship, drawing in large part on a longitudinal prospective study that we conducted at Cornell University's R. Brinkley Smithers Institute of Alcohol-Related Workplace Studies. In this 10-year research project, we focused on three blue-collar fields of employment: transportation, manufacturing, and construction. We chose these industries because of their permissive drinking cultures, which put employees at risk of developing alcohol-related problems. Our population comprised railroad workers, flight attendants, and urban transport workers (transportation); unskilled, semiskilled, and skilled assembly-line workers and machine operators (manufacturing); and skilled tradespeople, such as electricians and plumbers (construction).

We began our study by interviewing dozens of recent retirees from the three industries on their retirement experience. We also conducted several rounds of focus groups with other recent retirees and with employees who were soon to retire. In these open-ended interviews and focus group meetings, we discussed the retirees' work history, their experiences at work just prior to retirement, the reasons for their retirement, their activities since retirement, and their health history. We used these qualitative data to help identify the variables that we would investigate further using more quantitative methods and to help frame hypotheses regarding the nature of their influence on subsequent drinking behavior.

To construct our sample, we asked nine national and local unions representing workers in the three industries to provide contact information for employees who would be eligible to retire between May 2001 and February 2002. Using computer-assisted telephone interviewing, we began contacting those individuals around 6 months prior to the date they became eligible for retirement. Those who agreed to participate were then surveyed annually for the next 10 years. About half of those we contacted agreed to participate in the study—1,279 in all, including 882 men and 397 women (men made up 69% of the total). The respondents ranged in age from 43 to 70 at the project's start, with a mean age of 57 (the age range reflects differences in retirement eligibility from union to union).

During each telephone interview, respondents were asked a series of questions about their drinking over the last month and about other attitudes, behaviors, situations, and conditions that might be related to alcohol use. To capture the frequency and quantity of alcohol use, we asked respondents how many days in the last month they consumed an alcoholic beverage and how many drinks they tended to have at a time. To create a measure of periodic heavy drinking (binge drinking), we asked how many days over the last month they drank six or more drinks in a given day. Finally, we used the Drinking Problems Index to capture problem drinking (see Table 1.4). A full list of articles published or prepared on the basis of this longitudinal study appears in the Appendix.

The rest of this book will proceed as follows. In chapter 2, we will summarize theoretical arguments which suggest an association between retirement and increased or problem drinking. (Note that such associations are not always positive; some theoretical perspectives suggest a negative association between retirement and alcohol use, at least for some people.) Chapter 3 will briefly review the empirical literature on retirement and drinking and will describe some problems that limit the application of much of the extant research. Following this, chapters 4 and 5 will focus on the results of our 10-year study of retirement and its alcohol-related consequences in order to describe how conditions and relationships at work (chapter 4) and in retirement (chapter 5) influence drinking in retirement. In chapter 6, we will enlarge the discussion to touch briefly on other forms of substance abuse (i.e., illicit drugs and prescription medications) in late life in general and in relation to retirement in particular. Chapter 7 will describe some possible solutions for helping the troubled retiree, such as employer-based and peer-based assistance programs. Finally, in chapter 8 we will summarize our conclusions and offer some ideas for fruitful new lines of research.

NOTES

1. The National Health Interview Survey was designed by the National Center for Health Statistics, a department of the Centers for Disease Control and Prevention (CDC). It is administered by the US Census Bureau. The Behavioral Risk Factor Surveillance System is a telephone survey run by the CDC. The National Household Survey on Drug Abuse (now called the National Survey on Drug Use and Health) is sponsored by the Substance Abuse and Mental Health Services Administration (SAMHSA). Both the CDC and SAMHSA are agencies of the US Department of Health and Human Services.

CHAPTER 2

Theoretical Background

Over the years, scholars have drawn on theories from diverse fields to illuminate the potential link between retirement and drinking. The various theories each offer an approach to explaining why retirement might trigger or exacerbate drinking for some people and potentially diminish it for others.

In this chapter, we present six different theoretical perspectives that offer insights into this question: the stress and coping perspective, role theory, the social network approach, continuity theory, the social control perspective, and the life course approach. In presenting these frameworks in this order, we do not mean to imply that any one is more valid than any other, though the theories do differ in their scope and scale. It is perhaps most useful to think of them as offering six partial and overlapping pictures, each of which can inform our thinking about the subject in some way. Within this schema, the stress and coping perspective and the life course approach are the broadest and to some degree can be said to underlie (stress and coping) or frame (life course) the others.

THEORETICAL PERSPECTIVES THAT INFORM STUDIES OF RETIREMENT

Stress and Coping Perspective

The stress and coping perspective infuses nearly all the scholarly literature on retirement and drinking, including works grounded in other theoretical frameworks. The reasoning here is simple. Alcohol is, or may appear to be, a potent and readily accessible means of self-medication when individuals are faced with sources of stress they find difficult to cope with.

Retirement may itself offer relief from some key stressors, namely, those associated with the demands and challenges of work. Retirement may offer the promise of a permanent vacation, time to engage in leisure pursuits that previously had to be squeezed in during weekends, and an end to the tyranny of the alarm clock. But retirement also presents older adults with many potential new stressors, such as reduced income, a loss of salient roles or work identity, and a shrinking social network. Retirement is also the context within which older adults may experience other stressors not directly related to the exit from work, including declining physical health and strength (Kuerbis & Sacco, 2012). Moreover, that much-desired "permanent vacation" may eventually lose its luster as the pleasures of unlimited leisure time give way to a sense of marginalization, boredom, and empty hours.

According to the tension reduction hypothesis introduced by Conger (1956), stress may lead people to excessive drinking in two ways. First, alcohol may be used to dampen or dull the strain resulting from exposure to stressors. Second, it may be used to mitigate any experienced tension or strain resulting from the stress exposure. In the context of retirement, the former may mean, for example, that drinking—particularly drinking that serves as the basis for social interaction—is used as a way to fill those empty hours or at least lessen the loneliness, tedium, and sense of meaninglessness associated with the retirement experience. In the second case, alcohol may be used as a means to cope with strain manifested in the form of anxiety, depression, exhaustion, or pain (Kuerbis & Sacco, 2012).

Of course, how stressful the transition to retirement will be and how likely the individual will be to drink as a means to cope with such stress are both contingent upon a wide variety of individual and situational factors (e.g., personality traits, marital status, alcohol-related social norms) that influence the individual's vulnerability (Szinovacz, 2003). The theoretical approaches and perspectives described in this chapter all inform this issue of vulnerability in different ways.

Role Theory

Role theory, as its name suggests, emphasizes the importance of roles and role transitions in the retirement process (Kuerbis & Sacco, 2012; Wang, 2007). Specifically, the theory proposes that one strong influence on post-retirement adjustment is the degree to which the individual's sense of identity is built around preretirement employment roles, including organizational and career roles. Retirement means putting aside these old roles and adjusting to new ones—the roles of at-home spouse, parent, grandparent, or community member, on the one hand, and, potentially, new work roles (consultant, contract worker, second-career employee), on the other (Kuerbis & Sacco, 2012; Wang, 2007; Wang & Shultz, 2010). Retirees whose self-image and identity were constructed around their old work roles may find the adjustment to retirement difficult and stressful. They may feel marginalized and adrift and may have trouble establishing new goals and motivations. Conversely, individuals retiring from jobs they found stressful or burdensome may be pleased to be relieved of their work responsibilities and may transition smoothly into their new roles. The same goes for individuals who may have enjoyed their jobs but whose sense of self incorporates goals and values beyond the work world and who are glad for the opportunity to engage in other pursuits, such as spending time with family or volunteering (Wang, 2007; Wang & Shultz, 2010).

Applying this perspective to alcohol use, the degree to which retirement is experienced as a loss (of identity and meaning) or as a relief (from work responsibilities) can influence the retiree's drinking patterns. People who feel lost following retirement may turn to alcohol as a coping mechanism—a means of diverting the mind, relieving stress, or just passing the time. Those who experience retirement in terms of the freedom or opportunity to take on new roles are less likely to use alcohol in this way (Kuerbis & Sacco, 2012).

Social Networks

Social relationships influence all sorts of behavior, by establishing or transmitting a set of behavioral and attitudinal norms. Put more simply, people draw on their peers for cues about how to act in different circumstances. Social networks can thus have a direct effect on drinking behavior simply by transmitting how much and when it is deemed legitimate to drink. At the same time, social relationships can have an indirect effect on drinking, by amplifying or (more likely) reducing the effects of stress.

Looking at these effects from a slightly different angle, the loss-or-relief framework that we discussed in relation to pre- and postretirement roles can also be applied to the social networks that surround individuals at work. According to this perspective, retirement is accompanied by the loss of a critical base of social support, with retirees often being largely cut off from their work-based friendship and advice networks precisely when they are being confronted with the stresses of a major life transition (Perreira & Sloan, 2001). While retirees may remain in contact with their work friends, such ties are bound to be weakened with the reduced intensity of contact that often accompanies retirement. This is important because work-based ties and friendships serve as an important resource in helping individuals cope with stress in their lives, offering both emotional support (someone to talk to) and material or instrumental help (a loan when money is tight or the ability to absorb some of a troubled colleague's workload). In this way, such work-based friendships may serve to mitigate alcohol-based self-medication.

At the same time, retirement can be framed as a relief from a social network point of view, with retirees being able to disengage not only from the stresses and frustrations of work but also from work-based drinking subcultures (Ekerdt, De Labry, Glynn, & Davis, 1989). As we suggested when describing the direct effects of social networks on drinking, social support does not serve axiomatically as a coping resource but, rather, can be an enabling factor in alcoholism and drug use (Falkin & Strauss, 2003; Hagihara, Tarumi, & Nobutomo, 2003; Seeman & Anderson, 1983). Thus, the weakening of work-based friendships may increase the risk that vulnerable individuals will turn to alcohol in the absence of supportive social networks—but simultaneously may reduce the individual's reliance on alcohol where these work-based friendships centered around drinking.

In Bacharach, Bamberger, Cohen, and Doveh (2007), we frame the distinction between loss and relief in relation to social networks as one between changes in the depth and breadth of social support. That is, a positive association between retirement and the onset or exacerbation of alcohol problems may be explained by a decline in the depth of social support, where retirement isolates individuals from those friends who, in the past, would provide emotional or material help at times of need. A negative association between retirement and drinking, in turn, can be explained by shifts in the size or composition of the support network. Effectively, retirement can remove from the individual's social network those work-based friends who, true, might once have provided social support but who also might have tended to encourage heavy drinking.

Changes in social support networks can thus predict a positive relationship between retirement and drinking (the loss or depth-of-support mechanism) or a negative relationship (the relief or breadth-of-support mechanism). Alternatively, the two effects may be equally strong and thus cancel each other out, creating a null relationship. Whether one effect dominates the other and to what degree are likely to depend on various factors. Occupation is one: Certain occupations are known to have more permissive drinking cultures, making it likely—from a social network point of view—that the relief effect will dominate. Age and age-related factors are another. Broadly speaking, retirement can take place within a span of over three decades, with some "retiring" (though potentially continuing to work in a second career) in their 40s or 50s (e.g., police officers or members of the US armed forces) and others putting off retirement into their 70s or beyond. People's support networks change as they and their friends age, driven by factors like illness, the death of a spouse, or reduced mobility. Thus, the changes in social networks that accompany retirement may have a greater or lesser effect depending on whether the retiree is relatively young or older.

Continuity Theory

The notion behind continuity theory is that people tend to seek consistency in life patterns over time. The theory, developed by Robert Atchley (1989), holds that rather than looking toward transitions such as retirement in terms of the changes they are likely to bring about, individuals will aim to preserve and maintain existing structures, both internal (personality, beliefs, and values) and external (patterns of behavior, relationships, and social roles). To accomplish this, people apply "strategies tied to their past experiences of themselves and their social world" (Atchley, 1989, p. 183)—that is, their own previous experience and their knowledge and expectations derived from observing the social and cultural norms prevalent around them. In practice, this might mean continuing to work part-time after retirement or, alternatively, viewing retirement as a final career stage or as fulfillment of a goal (Kuerbis & Sacco, 2012; Wang, 2007).

In terms of drinking, continuity theory suggests that most retired people will continue to drink roughly as much or as little as they did prior to retirement. However, the theory also can be used to explain late-onset drinking problems, on the grounds that some people may be unable to accommodate major change or "discontinuity" without experiencing it as a stressful disruption (Wang, 2007). With regard to the issues raised in this volume, this might be especially likely when retirement takes place "off-time"—for instance, when employees are asked to take early retirement due to corporate restructuring or need to retire early because of their own or a loved one's ill health or physical disability. The continuity perspective also harmonizes with role theory, where people whose experiences and expectations centered around their work roles may not be psychologically prepared for the retired life. In these cases, people may find themselves developing new social relationships and lifestyle patterns, some of which may involve alcohol (Kuerbis & Sacco, 2012; Wang, 2007).

Social Control

In the realm of criminology, social control theory deals with ways in which people's relationships, commitments, and values help them achieve self-control and reject the temptation to engage in wrongful behavior. The theory, developed by Travis Hirschi, posits that as children grow up, parents and other authority figures (teachers, friends' parents, and other adults) help them internalize social norms and values both directly, by punishing bad behavior and rewarding good behavior, and indirectly, by exhibiting disappointment in response to bad behavior. The theory does not concern itself with what motivates people to commit wrongful acts but, rather, focuses on how socialization and social learning reduce the individual's propensity to engage in criminal behavior (Hirschi, 2002).

For adults, the regulatory roles once served by parents, teachers, and so on are filled by other social bonds, including those centered on the family, friendships, work, and religion (Moos, Schutte, et al., 2010). These social bonds motivate people to engage in behavior—including drinking behavior—that is deemed appropriate by relevant others (spouses, friends, or employers). Put differently, social control theory assumes that relevant others have an interest in preventing someone from drinking in a way that will affect his or her behavior or performance. Whether acting as authority figures or on the basis of caring, these individuals can inculcate norms mandating moderation in alcohol use both directly (e.g., by punishing infractions of workplace rules) and indirectly (e.g., by being upset when a spouse comes home drunk).

Crucially, social control theory suggests that a person's motivations for drinking are less important than whether or not the individual is able to limit his or her alcohol intake. Stress may precipitate drinking, in this view; but ultimately, the relevant issue is not whether someone drinks for this reason or that but whether the person's circumstances facilitate or impede self-control. In this regard, two elements of social control can enhance or reduce protection against excessive drinking. The first is visibility, that is, whether employers, family members, or others who might help are even aware there might be a problem. The second is whether those interested parties are willing and able to effectively intervene.

With regard to retirement, this line of reasoning leads to two conclusions. On the one hand, the work context places boundaries on drinking, both by limiting the time that can be devoted to drinking and by punishing drinking behavior (you'll lose your job if you continually show up late or intoxicated). In retirement, happy hour can start at 11:00 a.m. and continue into the wee hours (Adams, 1996). Social control theory thus suggests that retirement can be a risk factor for alcohol use. On the other hand, if the work context facilitates drinking behavior (i.e., if the workplace is characterized by a permissive drinking culture), being at home during the day may provide the kind of social control on drinking that was not found at work, at least for married/partnered retirees whose spouse or partner has also retired.

The Life Course Perspective

The life course perspective takes a long view, offering a means to consider retirement in the context of the entire life span. The framework assumes that individuals are subject to certain developmental trajectories from childhood through old age, comprising both structure-building (stable) and structure-changing (transitional) periods (Levinson, 1986). While the transitions and trajectories are, in a broad sense, constant from person to person, the shape of each one is contingent upon individual and contextual factors. With regard to the postretirement trajectory, the life course perspective predicts a gradual, ongoing "movement to activities and roles that involve less responsibility to others and less rigorous physical effort (i.e., leisure activities)" (Wang & Shultz, 2010, p. 178). Factors influencing the retirement transition involve the individual's personal history (e.g., how the person dealt with previous transitions or his or her work and leisure habits), individual attributes (e.g., gender, age, health, financial status, and skills), work-related characteristics (e.g., job status and career standing), and social factors (e.g., support networks and family obligations) (Szinovacz, 2003; Wang, 2007; Wang & Shultz, 2010).

The life course perspective is compatible with other theories, including the social control, stress reduction, continuity, and role theories, which offer insights into the mechanisms through which life course transitions such as retirement influence well-being (Szinovacz, 2003). For instance, the life course perspective emphasizes the interdependence of different life spheres, such that experiences in one sphere, like family, influence and are influenced by experiences in other areas, including work. Like role theory, the life course framework posits that retirees who recognized this interdependence while working and who are prepared to avail themselves of the alternative identities provided by nonwork spheres of life (spouse, grandparent, community member) are likely to enjoy greater psychological well-being after retirement (Szinovacz, 2003; Wang, 2007).

In keeping with the continuity perspective, the life course framework also stresses the importance of timing in transitions such as retirement. As we described, under the continuity model, people seek to maintain a stable self-concept as they go through life; and they accomplish this, in part, by anchoring their behavior and decisions to expectations derived from past experiences and social norms (Atchley, 1989). Role entries or exits that don't match the individual's goals or expectations vis-à-vis timing may be more disruptive than role transitions that are perceived to be on time (George, 1993; Wang, 2007). Shultz, Morton, and Weckerle (1998) reported empirical evidence for this, finding that workers who voluntarily retired early were more satisfied and rated themselves as healthier (both physically and mentally) than others who were forced into early retirement because of corporate restructuring. Of course, here as elsewhere, stress serves as the key underlying mechanism in such relationships. Many studies have shown an association between well-being and a sense of being in control of one's environment and actions (Szinovacz, 2003). Retirement is likely to be less stressful when it takes place within the context of previously adopted goals, choices, and expectations.

For our purposes, the most crucial insight offered by the life course framework may be its recognition that at any stage of life people's behavior is shaped by earlier events and choices. In the broad scheme of things, this implies that any choice which makes retirement more stressful might set the stage for alcohol misuse or drinking problems later in life (e.g., poor financial planning that leaves the retiree financially insecure). More directly, the pattern of alcohol use that a person develops earlier in life may carry over into the retirement years. For instance, alcohol misuse during middle age may result in alcohol dependence that continues beyond retirement. Equally, however, people who have struggled with alcohol for much of their lives and who have a history of trying to cut down and get sober may have an easier time doing so in retirement, when the stressors and (perhaps) drinking culture of the workplace are out of the picture.

AN INTEGRATED MODEL

One way of integrating these perspectives is by using what researchers call a "moderated mediation model." Moderated mediation models are

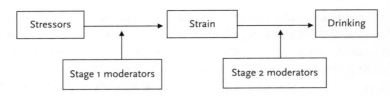

Figure 2.1:
Basic Model.

important in the etiology of alcohol misuse because they are able to capture the more complex interdependencies among the various risk and protection factors affecting drinking behavior (Frone, 2013). Such a model tries to explain the mechanisms that underlie the relationship between an independent variable (in this case, stressors) and a dependent variable (in this case, at-risk or problem drinking) by means of one or more intervening variables or mediators (in this case, strain). Further, the model aims to show how various moderating factors (such as aspects of the individual's personality, demographic profile, or environment) amplify or attenuate the relationships described by the mediated path. The basic model, first presented by Frone (1999), looks something like Figure 2.1.

Frone developed this model to elucidate how work-based stressors may be linked to workforce alcohol misuse. However, the same model may be easily applied to the question of how retirement-related stressors may precipitate or exacerbate alcohol misuse among older adults. To explain the processes captured by this model, we turn first to the mediation component and then to the moderation component.

Consistent with Conger's (1956) tension reduction hypothesis, the mediation component of Frone's (1999) model suggests that two mechanisms must be considered when trying to understand why individuals may turn to alcohol when encountering stressful situations or conditions. First, exposure to stressors may lead to drinking directly, such as when a bored or lonely retiree begins drinking to pass the time. This is represented by the path labeled "1" in Figure 2.2. However, stressors can also have an indirect or mediated effect on drinking, represented by the path labeled "2" in Figure 2.2. This path suggests that alcohol may be used to mitigate the tension or strain experienced as a result of exposure to stressors, such as when drinking serves to self-medicate anxiety, depression, or pain. To clarify how this differs from the direct path, let's return to the example suggested earlier. In the direct path, drinking serves as a direct response to boredom or loneliness: Drinking simply replaces the individual's previous

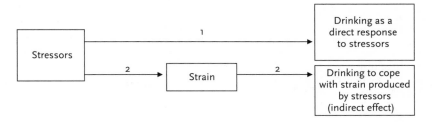

Figure 2.2:
Expanded Mediation Model.

activity (work). In the indirect path, boredom and loneliness may give rise to a deeper and more debilitating negative emotional state such as depression, anxiety, or stress, and the individual drinks because it makes him or her feel better or more at ease—at least for a while.

The stress and coping perspective described serves as the foundation of the moderated mediation model for retirement and alcohol use. The other five approaches offer variations on this basic theme, emphasizing different stressors and/or moderators, depending on the particular lens through which they view the retirement experience. For example, in terms of the differential emphasis placed on role stressors, while role theory emphasizes role loss as a key retirement-based stressor, the social network perspective emphasizes social isolation. The different approaches also suggest different types of conditioning factors (i.e., moderators), with stage 1 moderators operating to make a retired person more or less vulnerable to experiencing strain or tension as a result of those stressors and stage 2 moderators operating to make a retired person more or less vulnerable to drinking in order to reduce or mitigate this strain. In this sense, they offer important insights into just when, in what situations, and among whom we are likely to see these various risk factors have more or less of an effect on older adults' drinking behavior.

Putting this all together, we present moderated mediation models derived from each theoretical perspective. For the sake of simplicity, these models follow Frone's basic model (i.e., Figure 2.1), rather than the expanded version depicted in Figure 2.2.

The figures show graphically how different aspects of retirement generate potential stressors and how particular factors operate to influence the individual's psychological response, behavior, or both. For instance, the role theory model (Figure 2.3) shows that individuals who perceive their own value or identity as derived from the work realm will be more vulnerable to strain (e.g., anxiety or depression) following retirement than people who have developed robust goals and values outside of work. The

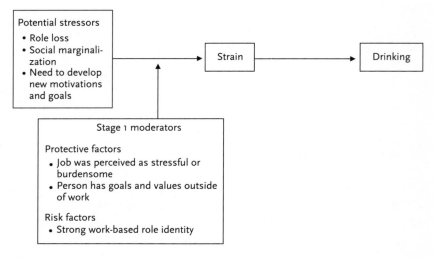

Figure 2.3:
Role Theory.

continuity theory model (Figure 2.5) emphasizes readiness for change as key to whether an individual will respond to retirement with resilience. The social network model (Figure 2.4) points to the role of nonwork friends and family as making the retiree more or less vulnerable to the social isolation that sometimes follows the departure from work. That figure adds a set of stage 2 moderators, showing that the drinking norms associated with

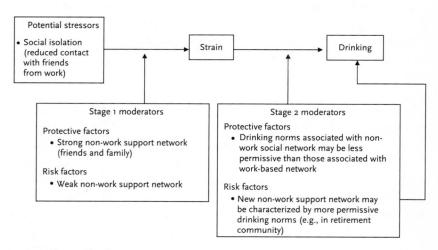

Figure 2.4:
Social Networks.

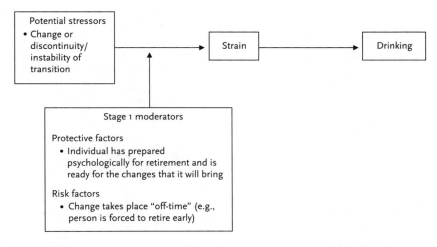

Figure 2.5:
Continuity Theory.

nonwork social networks can affect whether retirees respond to the strain related to social isolation by drinking. Figure 2.6, illustrating the social control model, adds to the picture the notion that friends, family members, or even a new work context (if the person is in bridge employment) may serve as a source of behavioral norms mandating moderation in alcohol use.

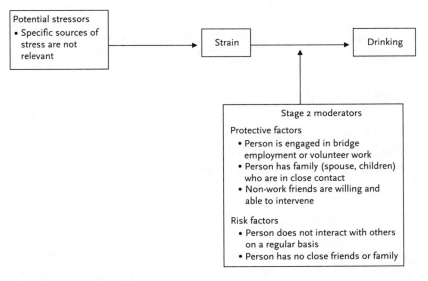

Figure 2.6:
Social Control.

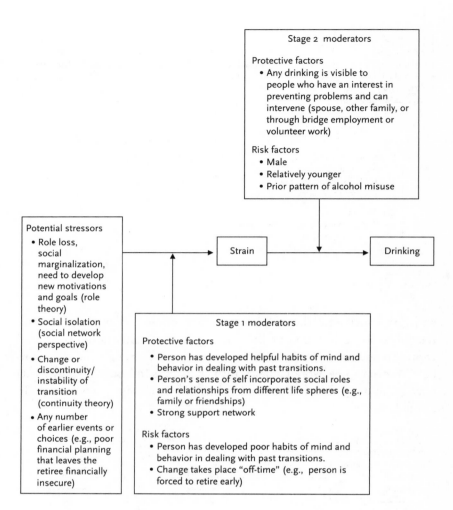

Figure 2.7:
Life Course Theory.

The life course model (Figure 2.7) could in theory include almost all the elements of the other models. Here, we include only key factors mentioned in this chapter, some of them derived from other models and some not.

SUMMARY AND CONCLUSION

As this chapter shows, the theoretical perspectives that have been applied to alcohol consumption and misuse in retirement suggest that the relationship between the two is complex and multifaceted. It is important to underscore that the various approaches are compatible rather than in competition and, indeed, sometimes complement each other (as when the role loss and social marginalization posited by role theory help explain why change can be stressful under continuity theory). What this means is that the goal of research on retirement and alcohol is not to determine which theories are "right" but to delineate when and under what conditions the many factors that influence drinking in retirement might come into play. From a practical perspective, such an understanding is important in that it provides us with vital insights into how, where, when, and among whom intervention resources should be invested. It also offers important clues as to the types of interventions that need to be developed, an issue that we will discuss further in chapter 7.

In the next chapter, we will begin to look at empirical evidence for the relationship between drinking and retirement. Given what we have seen to this point, the reader will be unsurprised that this evidence is not straightforward.

CHAPTER 3

Empirical Evidence for the Retirement–Drinking Relationship

In chapter 1, we showed that drinking in later life (i.e., beginning around the traditional retirement age) can be a serious problem and one that is becoming more important, from a public health perspective, as the population ages. In chapter 2, we described theoretical grounds for expecting that retirement has the potential to raise the risk of unhealthy or problem drinking for some people and lower it for others. In the current chapter, we will briefly review empirical studies conducted by ourselves and others that seek to answer how retirement—as a discrete event—may affect older adults' drinking behavior.[1] By retirement as a "discrete" event, we are referring to the more traditional conceptualization of retirement as the decision to permanently disengage from the workforce. While we are aware (as we pointed out in chapter 1) that retirees are increasingly choosing to transition into retirement via alternative paths, many of which involve remaining in the workforce in some form, social science research inevitably lags behind the phenomena it seeks to study, and so studies of the retirement–drinking relationship that take bridge employment into account are few in number. Accordingly, nearly all the studies that we review in this chapter either compare drinking among those "retired" with their peers still working or compare alcohol consumption or misuse for a cohort of older adults from the time they were employed to a given point in their retirement.

A REVIEW OF THE LITERATURE

According to Kuerbis and Sacco (2012), some 30-odd papers published in scholarly journals since the mid-1980s relate, in one way or another, to the association between retirement or work exit, on the one hand, and alcohol consumption, alcohol misuse, or alcohol-related problems, on the other. The majority of these papers examine how a variety of health-related outcomes (including alcohol consumption) may be associated with aging or shifts in work status. Accordingly, many of these studies relate to the retirement–alcohol relationship in only the most peripheral sense, with some even focusing strictly on participants who have yet to retire. Papers such as these will not be discussed in the current chapter. Instead, we will focus on studies that directly examine how the shift in work status from employed to retired may influence drinking behavior.

The papers that we review in this chapter tend to report on large-scale (i.e., large-sample) and often multiyear research projects. Such projects are necessary for several reasons. First, alcohol misuse is (gratefully) what scientists call a "low base-rate phenomenon," meaning that one needs a large sample in order to be able to reliably pick up how such phenomena vary in relation to some other factor. Second, among older adults, patterns of alcohol consumption and misuse are largely invariant in the short term and change only very slowly over time (Kerr, Fillmore, & Bostrom, 2002). This means that to capture shifting patterns of alcohol use/misuse, researchers are often best off applying a long-term (i.e., longitudinal) research design. Finally, to the extent that shifts do occur, they are likely to be initiated by a complex set of antecedent factors, potentially varying from one person to the next. Aside from further reinforcing the need for a large sample, this complexity means that researchers need to be able to collect data on a wide range of variables.

Despite the impressive nature of such massive projects, which require significant investment on the part of researchers and their (often government) sponsors, it is important to point out two broad limitations that mark many of these studies and that make it difficult to draw clear implications from them as a whole. The first is that many of these studies tend to draw their data from existing data sets on aging or retirement. For example, several studies examining the retirement–alcohol relationship analyze data from the University of Michigan's Health and Retirement Study, launched in 1992, which broadly aims to enhance our understanding of the decision to retire and its health-related consequences. Using a prospective or forward-looking study design, the Health and Retirement Study has surveyed over 26,000 Americans aged 50 or older every 2 years, collecting data about income, pensions, insurance, health and disabilities, and cognitive functioning. This broad, prospective coverage of retirement-related issues may not sound like a limitation, and, indeed, in most respects it is not. In fact, many of these larger data sets offer a tremendous advantage in that they tend to track participants over time, allowing us to see how shifts in situations or status influence subsequent health-related outcomes. On the other hand, because these studies cover such a broad range of issues, they tend to offer limited depth with regard to each one. For example, while substance use is a health-related consequence covered by such surveys, many of them collect data on modal consumption (i.e., typical frequency and quantity of consumption) only. Although such measures may be useful in identifying alcohol dependence (manifested in terms of consuming large quantities of alcohol on a consistent and frequent basis), they tend not to capture occasional alcohol misuse, for example, by not tracking periodic heavy drinking ("bingeing") or moderate consumption that may make it difficult for some individuals to function normally.

The second limitation is that these studies tend to be framed around the more traditional conceptualization of retirement as a discrete event. Such a conceptualization greatly simplifies the issue that researchers seek to address in that it narrows the question to how one's work status affects drinking behavior. On the other hand, such a conceptualization may be a rather artificial oversimplification, one which neglects the fact that there is an increasingly long transition phase through which individuals pass as they move from one status to another. We will discuss this issue in greater detail toward the end of this chapter. At this point, it is important to note that such a simple, dichotomous conceptualization forces scholars to categorize their participants as either employed in their career job or retired and thus disengaged from the workforce. How they make this call can obviously have a significant impact on a study's findings. Moreover, inconsistent categorization rules alone can result in findings that greatly diverge from one study to the next.

Given these two considerations, the empirical studies that we review in this chapter can hardly be expected to capture the complex interplay of antecedents and moderators suggested by the theoretical arguments discussed in chapter 2. Indeed, the evidence raised by these studies is highly equivocal: Some studies support a positive relationship between retirement and alcohol misuse, others support a negative relationship, and a third group of studies suggest a null effect. As we review the studies, we will highlight various issues specific to each that affect the validity of the findings or what we can learn from them. We will then draw from the present discussion to summarize possible reasons for the inconsistent findings. Finally, we will suggest a path toward harmonizing them, a path we will then follow in chapters 4 and 5.

Some of the key studies and their findings are summarized briefly in Table 3.1. Our own work is not included in this table, though we discuss two of our own studies in this chapter.

Table 3.1. SOME STUDIES ON THE RELATIONSHIP BETWEEN RETIREMENT AND ALCOHOL: POSITIVE, NEGATIVE, AND NULL EFFECTS

Study	Sample and method	Findings		
		Positive effects	Negative effects	Null effects
Ekerdt et al. (1989)	• US Department of Veterans Affairs Normative Aging Study • 416 male veterans, 24% retired • Time points: 2 • Time span: 2 years	Retirees more likely to report the onset of periodic heavy drinking and drinking problems		
Perreira & Sloan (2001)	• University of Michigan Health and Retirement Study • 7,731 community-dwelling seniors, 34% retired • Time points: 4 • Time span: 6 years	Retirement associated with increased alcohol consumption, both in the immediate wake of retirement and up to 4 years later		
Henkens et al. (2008)	• Mail-based survey in The Netherlands • 1,604 corporate and government employees, 55% retired • Time points: 2 • Time span: 6 years	Retirees reported greater increases in alcohol consumption than respondents who were still working. Increase in alcohol consumption following retirement greater for willing than unwilling retirees.		
Neve et al. (2000)	• Interviews and mail-based survey in The Netherlands • 1,327, 4% retired • Time points: 2 • Time span: 9 years		Retirement associated with a reduction in alcohol-related problems	
Rodriguez & Chandra (2006)	• University of Wisconsin National Survey of Families and Households • 7,599 healthy individuals aged 16 and over, 7% retired • Time point: 1		Retired men less likely than employed men to consume five or more drinks in 1 day	

(continued)

Table 3.1. (CONTINUED)

Study	Sample and method	Positive effects	Negative effects	Null effects
Brennan et al. (2010)	• In-person interviews • 595 community residents, 74% retired • Time points: 4 • Time span: 10 years		Frequency and quantity of drinking declined for all participants but especially for those who were retired. Effect disappeared when covariates added to the model.	
Midanik et al. (1995)	• Kaiser Permanente Retirement Study • 595 HMO members, 54% retired • Time points: 2 • Time span: 2 years			No significant differences in alcohol consumption or frequency of drunkenness
Platt et al. (2010)	• University of Michigan Health & Retirement Study • 6,787 community-dwelling seniors, 50% retired • Time points: 5 • Time span: 14 years			Alcohol consumption declined for most of the sample. No significant differences associated with retirement.

Note. HMO = health maintenance organization. Adapted from "The impact of retirement on the drinking pattern of older adults: A review," by A. Kuerbis and P. Sacco, 2012, *Addictive Behaviors, 37*, pp. 587–595.

Retirement as Promoting Alcohol Misuse or Problem Drinking

Several papers offer support for the notion that retirement may promote increased drinking or alcohol-related problems. In the oldest of these, Ekerdt et al. (1989) drew on data from the Normative Aging Study, an ongoing project established in 1963 by the US Department of Veterans Affairs, to analyze the effect of retirement on alcohol consumption. The authors looked at a subsample of data collected at two points in time (in 1982 and 1984) from a national sample of 416 male veterans, 100 of whom retired from their jobs during the study. When they analyzed the data for changes in alcohol consumption, they found that, as a group, those who retired did not differ from those who remained in the workforce—but there was greater variability among the retirees. Importantly, the retirees at time 2 were more likely to report the onset of periodic heavy drinking and drinking problems. However, as Kuerbis and Sacco (2012) point out, the study's age and sample composition limit its usefulness in predicting patterns for contemporary retirees. For instance, can we generalize from male veterans to nonveteran males? What about women? There are known cohort differences in alcohol consumption. Thus, retirement-related shifts in the drinking behavior of World War II vets may not be generalizable to their children, the Baby Boomers.

Perreira and Sloan (2001) used data from the University of Michigan Health and Retirement Study. The authors analyzed four waves of data for 7,731 individuals, 34% of whom retired during the study period (participants were aged 51–61 at the study's start and were almost equally divided between men and women). Retirement was associated with increased alcohol consumption, both in the immediate wake of retirement and up to 4 years later. The study's validity is somewhat limited by the fact that the final sample was not wholly representative of the larger population: for instance, less-educated, nonwhite men were more likely to drop out or die during the course of the study, as were heavy drinkers. In addition, the authors focused strictly on alcohol consumption (neglecting misuse or alcohol-related problems) and did so using only a general categorical variable (increase, decrease, or no change), in part to compensate for possible inconsistencies in measurement. Indeed, both key variables ("retirement" and "a drink") were poorly defined in the survey questionnaires and, thus, open to interpretation by participants. On the positive side, as noted by Kuerbis and Sacco (2012, p. 589), this study was one of only a few "to control for known predictors of changes in alcohol consumption in later life, thus allowing for a more rigorous test of the impact of retirement specifically on drinking behavior." Additionally, by examining alcohol use at two points following retirement, this study provides one of the first insights into the sustainability of retirement-related shifts in consumption. The authors found not only that consumption increased in the immediate period following work disengagement but also that this increase was still observable several years later.

Another study that offers rough support for a positive association between retirement and alcohol misuse is that of Henkens, van Solinge, and Gallo (2008). These authors analyzed data from 1,604 Dutch individuals, aged 50 to 64 at baseline, who were employed in 2001 in over 100 public and private enterprises; slightly more than half (55%) retired during the 6 years of the study. As in the case of Perreira and Sloan (2001), Henkens et al.'s analysis focused strictly on shifts in alcohol consumption. However, unlike Perreira and Sloan (2001), rather than examining actual shifts in self-reported consumption at varying points in time, Henkens et al. relied upon participants' accounts of how their drinking had changed, asking them to indicate whether their alcohol consumption had risen, fallen, or remained unchanged over the past 5 years. Although self-reports of alcohol consumption have been found to provide accurate and reliable accounts of drinking in the prior 1 to 4 weeks (Gruenewald & Johnson, 2006; Gruenewald & Nephew, 1994), self-reports of drinking in the more distant past, and all the more so reports of how drinking "then" compares to drinking "now," are likely to be tainted by current circumstances or behavior—what researchers call "retrospective bias."

Despite these methodological limitations, Henkens et al.'s study generated a number of interesting findings. In general, the researchers found that retirees reported greater increases in their alcohol consumption than respondents who were still working. But the researchers also differentiated between those reporting that their retirement was voluntary and those who said they felt they had to retire (e.g., for health reasons). The increase in alcohol consumption following retirement was greater for the willing than the unwilling retirees. However, the latter still reported a larger increase than those remaining employed, and they were less likely to report having reduced their consumption than those remaining at work. As the authors suggest, this pattern may have much to do with the health status of those who retired unwillingly. Assuming that health concerns influenced their decision to retire, they may have already been drinking less prior to retirement, making it unsurprising that any postretirement reduction in consumption would be less than for those remaining employed. On the other hand, assuming that some who retired unwillingly did so for reasons other than their health (e.g., because a spouse retired), the loss of employment-based controls might account for greater increases in consumption relative to those remaining employed.

In the context of our 10-year study of retirement and drinking described in chapter 1, we too explored this issue of how retirement as a discrete event may affect older adults' drinking behavior. In Bacharach, Bamberger, Sonnenstuhl, and Vashdi (2004), we looked specifically at the more immediate implications of retirement. That is, given that the impact of retirement on drinking when assessed over the longer term may be confounded by a variety of other factors, such as aging or declining health, we focused on shifts in drinking behavior that were more contemporaneous with the shift to retirement itself. Two additional aspects of our study are important. First, rather than examining work status as a dichotomous construct (i.e., retired or still working), we took into account that many older adults more accurately fall into the intermediary category of bridge employment described earlier. Second, we examined a variety of alcohol-related outcomes such as periodic heavy drinking (i.e., bingeing) as well as modal consumption.

As we described in chapter 1 the broader study from which the data for this initial paper were drawn, we won't detail the methodology here. Suffice it to say that in our 2004 paper we compared the drinking behavior of study participants 6 months after they became retirement-eligible to their drinking behavior 1 year previously. Our analysis was based on a final sample of 1,083 respondents (748 men and 335 women), of whom 263 (24%) were fully retired at time 2. The majority remained fully employed, and a small minority—30 respondents, or 3%—were engaged in bridge employment.

Overall, we found that alcohol consumption patterns remained relatively stable across time for all three employment groups (retired, bridge retired, and still employed). That is, neither of the two retirement trajectories examined (i.e., fully retired or bridge employment) was associated with a change from abstinence to consumption, with increased frequency of consumption, or with the emergence or exacerbation of a drinking problem. This is not surprising in that other studies indicate that patterns of alcohol consumption are fairly stable among older adults (Kerr et al., 2002). However, two findings depart from that pattern. First, relative to continued employment, bridge employment was associated with a significant increase in the average quantity of alcohol consumed per occasion (though the small sample size of those in bridge employment casts some doubt on the broader relevance of that finding). Second, participants who were fully retired at the end of the year were twice as likely as those who remained fully employed to engage in periodic heavy drinking. This was true even when we controlled for periodic heavy drinking at baseline, meaning that a subgroup of participants began to engage in binge drinking sometime during the year of the study.

This second finding raises an interesting question. Leaving aside the subgroup that began to engage in binge drinking after the first data collection, it is possible that, in some cases, retirement may be more a consequence of drinking problems than a cause of them. That is, it may be that those most likely to retire immediately on becoming eligible are precisely those reporting a greater number of drinking problems prior to retirement.

Those individuals may seek to lower the risk of being dismissed without benefits by opting to retire at the first opportunity. Indeed, we found that respondents who were fully retired reported more drinking problems prior to becoming retirement-eligible (i.e., at time 1) than those continuing to work. These findings are in keeping with those of Perreira and Sloan (2001), who also found retirement to be most frequently associated with increased drinking among those with a preretirement history of problem drinking. The findings suggest that the assumed causal link of retirement serving as an antecedent to problem drinking cannot always be taken for granted.

Retirement as Reducing Alcohol Misuse or Problem Drinking

A number of other studies suggest that retirement may reduce alcohol consumption or at-risk and problem drinking. For example, Neve, Lemmens, and Drop (2000) used data from a 9-year longitudinal study in The Netherlands to examine changes in alcohol use and alcohol-related problems associated with role changes at different stages of life, including retirement. An analysis of data including weekly average alcohol consumption, frequency of heavy drinking, and scores from the Drinking Problems Index produced only one significant finding vis-à-vis retirement: Among those who consumed alcohol, retirement was associated with a reduction in alcohol-related problems. However, the authors failed to take into account the possible confounding effect of age. Accordingly, the negative impact of retirement on alcohol-related problems may be largely spurious, with retirement simply reflecting the impact of aging and/or the health-related problems that often accompany it.

Rodriguez and Chandra (2006) analyzed data from the National Survey of Families and Households, conducted by the Center for Demography at the University of Wisconsin. Their data (dating to the late 1980s and early 1990s) related to 7,599 healthy individuals aged 16 or over, of whom 532 were retired. Although their primary focus in this study was on the link between the receipt of social benefits (e.g., welfare) and alcohol use and misuse, their models incorporated employment status variables such as retirement. Unlike the studies described previously, theirs is a cross-sectional study, comparing consumption levels among different categories of men and women. Their findings indicate no difference between employed and retired women with respect to any alcohol-related outcome. However, the authors did find that retired men were significantly less likely than men who were employed full-time to misuse alcohol (defined here as consuming five or more drinks in the same day). Unfortunately, once again, the authors failed to fully account for the possible confounding effect of age (although they did rerun their analyses after dividing their sample into those 40 and younger and those older than 40; the results remained stable across the two groups). Accordingly, it is highly probable that what appears to be a retirement effect is in fact an age effect stemming from the tendency of heavy drinking to decline in older age, as we described in chapter 1.

Most recently, Brennan, Schutte, and Moos (2010) examined the role of retirement in shaping drinking trajectories over a 10-year period. They analyzed data from 595 participants from a community sample, of whom 443 were retired and 152 were working throughout the study period (participants' mean age at the study's start was 62). The authors found that for all participants the frequency of drinking declined moderately over the study period and that this decline was especially marked for those who were retired. However, consistent with the suspicions noted regarding several prior studies, they found that this effect disappeared once other variables, such as health and income, were added to the model: Poorer health and lower incomes at baseline predicted a steeper decline in drinking frequency, as did the presence of current drinking problems. The authors concluded that baseline health, income, and problem-drinking history are more important than whether or not someone is retired for predicting long-term drinking patterns.

Despite their methodological problems, these studies, taken as a group, cast significant doubt on the conventional wisdom that retirement, as a dysphoric event, prompts individuals to drink more or more hazardously. Indeed, these studies are compatible with the idea that, for many, retirement may be a positive life change, offering relief from many of the work-based stressors that may have motivated heavy consumption or misuse in the past. However, as pointed out by Brennan et al. (2010), findings suggestive of a beneficial effect of retirement on drinking may in fact simply reflect other life changes contemporaneous with retirement (such as reduced income or declining health). Another possibility is that the impact of retirement on drinking is context-dependent. That is, retirement may have different effects on different people, depending upon their background or on the general situation in which they find themselves. We explore both of these options in the remaining sections of this chapter.

Retirement as Having No Effect on Alcohol Misuse or Problem Drinking

Null findings in the social sciences tend to be underreported in scholarly journals, for two reasons. First, null findings are apt to offer little "news."

Second, it is impossible to determine whether null findings truly reflect the absence of a relationship or whether methodological problems simply made some real relationship impossible to capture. Such methodological problems include poor measures, unrepresentative samples, and a failure to search for the relationship in the right context or under the necessary conditions. Nevertheless, null findings with regard to the retirement–alcohol relationship have been consistently reported, and this consistency may make them meaningful.

Midanik, Soghikian, Ransom, and Tekawa (1995) examined the impact of retirement on drinking and alcohol problems as part of the Kaiser Permanente Retirement Study, a longitudinal study aimed at assessing the impact of retirement among members of the Kaiser Permanente managed care consortium. The authors compared the mental health and health behaviors of 320 Kaiser Permanente members who retired during the 2-year study period (1985–1987) and 275 counterparts who did not. No differences emerged between the groups in consumption of alcohol or frequency of drunkenness. However, as the study sample was drawn from individuals who were able to maintain their membership in a health maintenance organization even following retirement, participants were relatively both more educated and more financially comfortable than the larger population. In addition, as in most of the other studies noted, retirement was treated as a dichotomous variable, leaving open the possibility that some participants had begun transitioning out of the workforce during the study period by engaging in bridge employment.

Platt et al. (2010) report findings from the Health and Retirement Study after 14 years of data collection (1992–2006). Their study covers 6,787 individuals, about half of whom retired during the study period. Based on data collected over at least five and up to eight time points, participants were categorized according to five drinking trajectories: abstainers, steady drinkers, increasing drinkers, decreasing drinkers, and sporadic drinkers. In general, alcohol consumption declined for most of the sample. Those participants who showed an increase in consumption were more likely to be well-educated, affluent, male, white, unmarried, less religious, and in good health; a history of problem drinking at baseline was also associated with increased alcohol use. Interestingly, unlike Perreira and Sloan (2001), who found an increase in alcohol consumption following retirement based on data from that study's first 6 years, Platt et al. (2010) found no such association. However, this study has several weaknesses, including the fact that the definition of *retirement* used in the study was unclear.

Finally, using data collected from the first three waves of our seven-wave study described in chapter 1, we sought to examine the impact of retirement on drinking behavior specifically among those who, prior to retirement, reported a baseline history of problem drinking (Bacharach et al., 2007). As the vast majority of those meeting this criterion were male, we excluded the handful of women in the subsample from our analyses. Accordingly, our analysis compared 71 men from the larger sample who reported a history of problem drinking with 236 fellow male study participants who did not have such a history. Overall, we found that retirement had no independent effect on the severity of drinking problems among the participants at a 2-year follow-up (though, as in nearly all the studies discussed already, in this study we did not consider the possible confounding effects of bridge employment, defining *retirement* based only on whether participants were receiving retirement benefits). More importantly, we found evidence that the impact of retirement on drinking problems may vary depending upon the alcohol-related norms—permissive or prohibitive—prevalent in the workplace from which the individual retires. It is precisely the role of such conditioning effects in explaining the inconsistent results noted to which we turn next.

EXPLAINING THE INCONSISTENCIES

Several factors may account for the inconsistent findings between the studies discussed in the preceding sections. The most important of these are listed in Table 3.2.

First, inconsistencies may stem from conceptual or methodological differences across studies. In this regard, how researchers define and measure retirement—and, in particular, how they handle the increasing proportion of workers who fail to completely disengage from the labor force while officially retiring and taking retirement benefits—can directly influence study outcomes. Once, retirement was a dichotomous variable with a fairly stable meaning: One day you were employed, most likely working full-time and bringing home a weekly paycheck; the next day you were retired and your working life was behind you. Today, many so-called retirees continue to work part-time or even full-time, and sometimes even for their old employer, while receiving retirement benefits. The effects of such bridge employment on workers' stress levels, social environment, financial stability, and so on may influence whether and how their drinking patterns change. As a result, inconsistencies or lack of clarity in how different studies define their samples and code participants' work status makes it difficult to draw conclusions or integrate findings from different studies.

Table 3.2. POSSIBLE REASONS FOR INCONSISTENT FINDINGS BETWEEN
STUDIES ON RETIREMENT AND ALCOHOL USE

Type of problem	Relevance to studies on retirement and alcohol use
Conceptual and methodological differences in defining independent variables	How is retirement defined and measured? Does it take into account the possibility of bridge employment or encore careers?
Inconsistent outcome measures	Does the study measure modal consumption (quantity and frequency)? Alcohol misuse (e.g., bingeing)? Dependence or alcohol use disorder? Problem drinking?
The omitted variable problem	Does the study take into account the possible confounding effects of other variables that change over time, such as age, income, and health status?
Representativeness of sample	Does the study account for the possibility that relationships found are contingent on a particular context or relevant to a particular study population? Are the findings generalizable?

Inconsistencies may also arise from the use of inconsistent outcome measures. Studies may measure modal alcohol consumption (the quantity and frequency of drinks consumed), alcohol misuse (bingeing or drinking to intoxication), dependence, or problem drinking (drinking to the point that it causes social or health problems). While a number of studies operationalize drinking in terms of a range of outcome measures (e.g., Bacharach et al., 2004; Ekerdt et al., 1989; Neve et al., 2000), others rely on vague or more limited measures (e.g., Henkens et al., 2008; Perreira & Sloan, 2001). This, too, impedes our ability to draw wide-ranging conclusions from many findings.

Further inconsistencies may emerge as a function of how researchers build and test their models. One of the biggest problems plaguing research on the retirement–drinking relationship is what researchers call the "omitted variable problem." This problem results from the testing of hypotheses without taking into account possible confounding effects of other related variables. In the brief review given here, we highlighted a number of such possible confounds, including age, (declining) income, and health status. Models that fail to control for the effects of aging or health on drinking patterns may identify an influence of retirement where none exists or may fail to observe such an influence if one is present. Here, it is important to remember that the effects of aging on alcohol use are themselves not clear-cut. In chapter 1 we pointed out that while by most accounts people tend to drink less as they grow older, some studies have found the opposite, suggesting that the relationship between drinking and aging is not linear. Yet while such uncertainty further clouds the picture with regard to retirement, the more significant concern is with the likely confound.

Overall, the failure to account for the effect of age and/or health on alcohol use, misuse, or problems when testing for the effect of retirement means that some of what appears to be an effect of retirement may in fact be spurious, having little to do with retirement at all. The greater the time that has passed since the individual retired, the more true this is. Thus, while individuals who have been retired for 20 years may drink less than when they were employed or less than those still working, it is impossible to attribute this decline or difference strictly to their retirement. In general, the fact that some studies statistically control for some of these potential confounds while others do not is likely to serve as a key source of methodological inconsistency.

Finally, as noted earlier, the relationship between retirement and alcohol may also be bounded or conditional, contingent upon the context within which retirement occurs. Sampling differences across studies often provide clues about such conditions, such as when an association is found between retirement and drinking in one type of sample but not in another. For example, as we discussed in chapter 1 when introducing our own study, certain blue-collar occupations have been identified as having more permissive drinking cultures, making employees in those fields more likely to be heavy drinkers and/or to develop drinking problems (Bacharach, Bamberger, & Sonnenstuhl, 2002; Frone, 2013). To the extent that consumption patterns among older individuals are relatively stable (Kerr et al., 2002), such occupational differences are likely to carry over into retirement. In addition, blue-collar retirees may be more likely than their white-collar counterparts to use alcohol as a means of self-medicating the strain induced by retirement-related financial stress (Ruben, 1992). Thus, studies including a greater number of blue-collar workers might uncover alcohol-related retirement effects that studies with a higher proportion of white-collar workers might not find.

This is just one example of a conditioning factor, with others suggested by the research reviewed earlier. For example, some of the findings described in this chapter suggest that the retirement–drinking relationship is contingent upon postretirement activity or work involvement, with our own research (Bacharach et al., 2004) indicating differences in outcomes for those fully versus partially retiring. Still, for every moderator tested or suggested to date, there are likely to be numerous others—such as a spouse's work status or a history of prior drinking problems—that have yet to be examined.

A NEW APPROACH

The equivocal findings on alcohol and retirement have a lot in common with other research on retirement and its effects. Studies have found positive, negative, and null relationships between retirement and a range of outcomes, including physical health, stress levels, depression, loneliness, life satisfaction, and physical activity (Wang, 2007). This is despite the fact that the adaptation to retirement has been the focus of extensive empirical study over recent decades (Wang, 2007). Indeed, one might be forgiven for thinking that scholars still have very little understanding of the processes by which individuals adjust to the shifts in their physical, social, financial, and other circumstances that invariably occur along with both aging and the withdrawal from work life that typically accompanies it.

What all this suggests is twofold. First, to understand the relationship between retirement and drinking, that relationship needs to be considered independently from the effects of aging on alcohol use. Second, the impact of retirement on alcohol use is likely to play out as part of a broader pattern by which individual retirees follow different retirement transition and adjustment processes. In other words, any effort to associate patterns of drinking (or any other outcome) to retirement must take account of a broad range of factors—sociodemographic characteristics, personality traits, work-related factors, other life events (e.g., death of a spouse)—that might help shape the individual's retirement experience.

Drawing on the theories discussed in chapter 2, the psychologist Mo Wang (2007) argues that well-being in retirement is likely to follow one of three trajectories. Wang describes findings that support these hypothesized trajectories based on an analysis of data from the Health and Retirement Study described in chapter 3. The analysis covers five waves of data dating from 1992 through 2000 for two sets of respondents: 994 who retired between the first and second waves and 1,066 who retired between waves 2 and 3.

In the first trajectory, which Wang terms the "maintaining pattern," psychological well-being is relatively high to begin with and remains so both during the passage from work to retirement and then into postretirement life. Wang argues that retirees who follow the maintaining pattern are likely to be those who successfully integrate retirement into their self-concept and lifestyle, as suggested by continuity theory. This might be by, for example, engaging in bridge employment. Others who are likely to follow the maintaining pattern include people who engaged in careful retirement planning or who are able to replace the companionship of work colleagues with that of a spouse.

The other two trajectories described by Wang also point, ultimately, to a stable and comfortable state of well-being for retirees. That is, with the passage of time, retirees should enjoy their postretirement life more and more, as predicted by the life course perspective (Wang, 2007, p. 457). The two trajectories differ in their paths during and in the immediate wake of the retirement transition. The first of these is the recovering pattern, in which well-being rises steeply at first, then gradually levels off and stabilizes over time. As implied by role theory, retirees who follow the recovering pattern are likely to include those whose jobs were stressful, physically demanding, or unpleasant in some other way.

The third and final trajectory forms a U-shaped pattern, in which well-being initially drops steeply and then gradually rises, eventually stabilizing at or above the level where it stood prior to retirement. Retirees likely to follow this pattern include those whose self-concept centered around work-related roles (as per role theory) or who, for other reasons, find retirement disruptive to their sense of self as constructed around events and expectations from the past (as per continuity theory). Still others may simply have unrealistic expectations about postretirement life. Wang's results suggest that three groups of retirees are particularly susceptible to the U-shaped pattern: those with declining health, those in unhappy marriages, and those who retired earlier than they had planned or expected. (Wang's analyses did not bear out this hypothesized pattern for two further groups: those facing financial insecurity and those who ultimately retired later than planned or expected.) In such cases, Wang suggests, retirees over time reevaluate their retirement experience, accept the limitations of their current status, and refocus their energies on adjusting to it, at which point measures of their well-being will improve.

This line of thought suggests that, rather than examining retirement as a discrete event and testing for how this event affects alcohol consumption, misuse, or problems, it makes more sense to frame retirement as an adjustment process, with different experiences or situations in retirement having diverse effects on these alcohol-related outcomes. In the following two chapters we will do just that, drawing on our own 10-year research project as well as the work of others to identify and illuminate some of the key issues at play. In chapter 4, we will discuss ways in which conditions and relationships at work (e.g., job satisfaction, workplace stress, or characteristics of work-based social networks) may influence drinking in retirement. In chapter 5, we will turn to the influence of conditions and relationships in retirement, looking at such variables as marital and financial stress. In both chapters, the trajectories suggested by Wang (2007) will serve as a useful point of departure for these considerations.

NOTES

1. We are indebted in this chapter to Alexis Kuerbis and Paul Sacco, whose recent review of the literature (Kuerbis & Sacco, 2012) presents a concise yet comprehensive summary of the most important theoretical and empirical research in this area.

CHAPTER 4

How Conditions and Relationships at Work Influence Drinking in Retirement

In chapter 3, we discussed three possible trajectories of psychological well-being during the retirement transition and adjustment process, as suggested by Wang (2007). In the maintaining pattern, well-being is relatively high to begin with and remains so throughout the transition from work to retirement and then into postretirement life. In the recovering pattern, well-being rises steeply at first, then gradually levels off and stabilizes. The U-shaped pattern begins with a steep initial drop in well-being, followed by a gradual rise.

As Figure 4.1 shows, all three trajectories converge over time toward the same stable and comfortable state of well-being. Where the lines diverge most sharply is at and immediately following their starting points—that is, prior to retirement and during the earliest stages of the retirement transition. This period is the main interest of this chapter.

Figure 4.1 captures graphically something that we have already pointed out several times in this volume, namely, that while retirement may be stressful or dysphoric for some, it is precisely the opposite for others. So one key to understanding just when or for whom retirement is likely to be linked with increased or problematic drinking involves identifying those factors that explain when retirement is likely to be stressful or dysphoric (i.e., stage 1 moderators in the moderated mediation model proposed in chapter 2). Clearly, many of these factors will be related to the retirement experience itself or to conditions and relationships exclusive

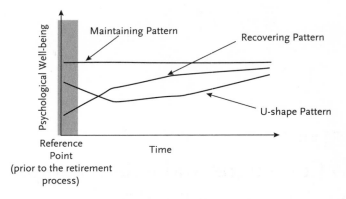

Figure 4.1:
Patterns of Change in Psychological Well-Being During the Retirement Transition and Adjustment Process.
Source: Wang, M. (2007). Profiling retirees in the retirement transition and adjustment process: Examining the longitudinal change patterns of retirees' psychological well-being. *Journal of Applied Psychology, 92*(2), 457.

to postretirement life. But others are likely to go back to conditions and relationships at work, and it is these that we will seek to illuminate in this chapter.

THE ROLE OF WORK-RELATED MODERATORS: INSIGHTS FROM RECENT RESEARCH

This chapter will examine various potential work-related moderators for the retirement–drinking relationship. Specifically, we will focus on studies that examine whether workplace conditions and relationships—such as workplace stress and workplace social networks—are likely to affect whether and to what degree retirement is perceived as dysphoric. At the same time, the studies we will discuss introduce a new element into the equation: the possibility that other moderating factors—for instance, other workplace conditions or perhaps individual attributes such as personality traits, demographic profile, values, or personal history—might interact with these workplace conditions and relationships to influence the strength or direction of their moderating effect. In other words, the effect of retirement on stress is moderated by some work condition, but for some definable set of individuals this moderating effect may be stronger or weaker or may be positive rather than negative (or vice versa). This is what researchers call a "three-way interaction," where a relationship between an independent variable (here, retirement) and a moderating variable (e.g., a work-related variable) varies in relation to a third variable (e.g., another work-related variable or an individual attribute) to affect an outcome (strain).

A brief example will illustrate the point. One factor that stands out as potentially influencing stress in retirement is job satisfaction. It seems reasonable to assume that people who perceive their work as unpleasant, stressful, or burdensome will experience retirement as a relief, while people who derive pleasure and satisfaction from their jobs will experience retirement as a loss. But on second thought, this conclusion is not obvious at all. Perhaps some people are simply more disposed to experience life in negative terms and others to focus on the positive aspects of whatever circumstances they are in. Perhaps the world really is divided into glass-half-empty, glass-half-full types. Yet these two assumptions lead to completely opposite conclusions: "low job satisfaction produces retirement-as-relief" versus "low job satisfaction implies retirement-as-dysphoria." And, indeed, "low job satisfaction produces retirement-as-relief" fits the recovering pattern in Wang's schema, while the obverse of these statements— "high job satisfaction produces retirement-as-loss" and "high job satisfaction implies retirement-as-pleasure"—fit the maintaining and U-shaped patterns. But who is likely to follow which pattern? The only way to begin to work out what role variables such as job satisfaction really play in the equation we're constructing is to examine how individual attributes and other factors interact with such variables to produce particular outcomes.

But what factors should we look at first? Here, one important source of information is the experiences of retirees themselves—or, in other words, ethnographies of retirement. As described in chapter 1, we began our own study by interviewing recent retirees about their experiences, health, reasons for retirement, and drinking behavior. Several factors emerged in one interview after another, suggesting that these were of potential significance for the questions of whether and when retirement is perceived as dysphoric and when such dysphoria might be translated into risky or problematic drinking. For example, many interviewees expressed sadness that their friendships with work colleagues had suffered since they retired. "These relationships kinda all died," said Ray, a former toolmaker and safety representative at an automobile factory. "My whole job was social." Another retiree, Joel—also formerly employed in automobile manufacturing—had similar feelings: "That's the only thing I miss about the place— the people." The link between socialization at work and drinking was also prominent. For instance, as Ray put it, "It's tough. Everyone is still working and you can't hit the joints with them 'cause you're not there anymore."

Another factor that stood out in the interviews was the importance of retirement agency—that is, whether the employee was happy to retire or felt that he or she was forced into retirement. In some cases, the push to retire seemed to come from the organization. For instance, Mary Jo, a railway mechanic and equipment inspector, said that before she retired she was sensing "a signal to leave...[It's] not the kind of work environment you want to stay in longer than necessary." Marc, a security officer for the same railway who was still working at the time of the interview, concurred: "I definitely get a feeling that they want me out." In other cases, the push to retire derived more from the employee's own concerns, for example, over failing health. Ray, the toolmaker and safety rep quoted above, who has emphysema, said he "wanted to work a couple more years, but my health forced me out." In this respect, as in others, different retirees we interviewed reported very different reactions to similar circumstances. For instance, Laurence, a steamfitter, retired because a business slowdown meant he wasn't working steadily. He could "see the writing on the wall" that business wasn't going to pick up and so made a virtue of necessity; yet he was not ready to retire, and his frustration is evident in his recorded interview. On the other hand, another steamfitter (Dan) also retired because he was laid off and wasn't working, yet he felt "it was time" and was very happy to leave.

The stories told by the recent retirees who we interviewed played a major role in shaping the nature of our 10-year project described in chapter 1. They informed the types of variables on which we sought to collect quantitative data and ultimately influenced the analyses that we ran on these data. We draw from the results of several of these analyses (and the studies that we built around them), along with relevant work from others, in the rest of this chapter.

We first highlight three studies—two of them our own—that examine how different interactions between work-related factors and individual-level variables affect the retirement–drinking relationship: workplace stress and gender, job satisfaction and retirement agency, and workplace social networks and a history of problem drinking. We then look at a fourth study in which we examine the interaction between two workplace variables considered in this context for the first time: unit-level drinking norms and unit-level stress climate. Finally, we describe another of our published works, in which we examine the potential moderating role of alcohol-related expectations in the retirement–drinking relationship.

This sort of research is just in its infancy, and we make no claim to offer comprehensive answers here. But the remainder of this chapter (and chapter 5) will offer a taste of the directions this sort of thinking can take us.

Workplace Stress and Gender

Before we consider workplace stress, it's worth devoting a few words to what the literature has to say about the moderating role of gender and other sociodemographic characteristics in the association between retirement and drinking behavior. According to Brennan et al. (2010), there has been only "limited investigation of demographic and personal characteristics that may account for or moderate the relationship between retired status and late-life drinking trajectories" (p. 165). However, the evidence that does exist (from Ekerdt et al. [1989], our own work, and other studies) suggests that marital status, race or ethnicity, education, and preretirement job level do not moderate the effects of retirement on drinking behavior in later life. The evidence for moderating effects of age, gender, health, and income, though, is more equivocal (Brennan et al., 2010). We'll limit our remarks to gender, which, besides being our main object of interest here, can highlight the immaturity of this literature as a whole.

There is some evidence that gender moderates the effect of retirement on drinking—in other words, that the experience of retirement, and its effects on drinking behavior, may differ for men and women. But in which direction? A few studies seem to suggest that retirement may have a protective effect for men but not for women. But the findings on gender from those studies are statistically weak or limited. For instance, Neve et al. (2000) found that while both men and women showed a slight increase in periodic heavy drinking after retirement, the figures for overall alcohol consumption seemed to fall for retired men but to rise for retired women. However, the number of women sampled (10 retired and 9 still working) was too small to draw any real conclusions about those groups. Rodriguez and Chandra (2006), in keeping with Neve et al. (2000), found higher monthly consumption among retired compared with employed women. But, in contrast to Neve et al. (2000), they found less likelihood of periodic heavy drinking for retired men compared to men who were still working. Meanwhile, the Kaiser Permanente Retirement study described in chapter 3 (Midanik et al., 1995) seems to show a protective effect of retirement for women but not for men. As we described in that chapter, Midanik and her colleagues found no effect of retirement on drinking behavior, as measured in terms of either alcohol consumption or frequency of drunkenness. However, retired women—but not retired men—were less likely to report drinking problems than their counterparts who remained employed.

These equivocal findings remind us, yet again, that a clear (or at least clearer) picture of any complex relationship is likely to arise not from investigating one variable in isolation, or yet from examining large numbers of variables simultaneously, but rather from studies that probe different sets of variables in relation to each other. With regard to the drinking–retirement relationship, one such study is that of Richman, Zlatoper, Zackula Ehmke, and Rospenda (2006), who explored the lingering effect of workplace stress on postretirement drinking behavior.

Richman and her colleagues examined three sets of conditions that can create a stressful work environment: sexual harassment, generalized workplace abuse, and psychological workload. Sexual harassment was measured by 19 items that assessed unwanted sexual attention, sexual coercion, and other unwelcome verbal or physical behavior of a sexual nature. Generalized workplace abuse was measured by 29 items designed to capture patterns of intimidating or humiliating behavior or verbal abuse. Psychological workload was measured by nine items reflecting a sense of needing to work "faster" or "harder."

The authors used mail surveys to contact 1,654 nonabstaining individuals (918 women and 736 men) who were employed by an urban midwestern university in 1996, when the first wave of data were collected; the respondents represented a variety of occupations, including faculty members, clerical staff, and maintenance or service workers, and were in their 20s through 60s at the study's start. Data were collected at four points over a 6-year period, during which time 71 respondents retired (6% of the sample). (*Retirement* was not defined in the study, leaving open the possibility that some of the retired respondents were engaged in bridge employment.) The authors analyzed the data both longitudinally (assessing the extent to which sexual harassment, generalized workplace abuse, and psychological workload experienced while working were associated with the frequency and quantity of drinking at wave 4) and cross-sectionally (assessing the extent to which retirees' drinking levels differed from those of current employees experiencing similar stress levels and of other retirees who had not experienced those stressors). Finally, they analyzed the extent to which gender moderated these relationships.

The analyses showed that, indeed, the effects of workplace stress on drinking outcomes appear to continue even after the individual has left the workforce. That is, overall, retirees who had experienced high levels of stress drank more than their counterparts who were still employed (and who were still experiencing a stressful workplace). This pattern held even in relation to a comparison between stressed and nonstressed workers, where stressed workers drank more than nonstressed workers but previously stressed retirees drank the most. The authors suggest that one explanation for this finding may involve the constraining role of workplace social controls. Workplace norms and regulations may inhibit the use of alcohol as a means of self-medication in response to highly stressful experiences. Retirement removes the stressful work experiences, but the strain induced by exposure to them takes longer to go away. At the same time, retirement also removes the social controls that limited drinking while the individual was in the workforce.

Importantly, though, the patterns differed somewhat for men and women. For women, high levels of all three measures of stress produced the pattern described above. But for men, this was true only for high levels of sexual harassment and generalized workplace abuse, while for high psychological workload, drinking was lower among retirees than among workers. Meanwhile, for low levels of stress (as measured by generalized workplace abuse and psychological workload), male retirees drank more than male workers but female retirees drank less than their working counterparts. The authors posit that retired women may experience greater strain from new role burdens than men do as women may bear the brunt of responsibilities such as caring for ill spouses or elderly parents or helping their own grown children with child care. If this is the case, women who retire from highly demanding jobs may have to deal with the strain from new or increased nonwork role burdens on top of the persisting strain from their former work roles. Thus, women who exit workplaces where stress levels were high may be at special risk for detrimental drinking outcomes.

The authors point out that one weakness of their study is the relatively small number of retirees in the sample. In addition, most had only been retired for 1 or 2 years at the study's end, when the drinking data were collected. Thus, the study sheds light only on the early stages of postretirement life (the start of the trajectories in Wang's figure, as we pointed out above). Nonetheless, this research is significant in that it points to a lingering impact of workplace stress on alcohol consumption even after retirement, especially for women, who physiologically are most at risk from drinking in excess.

Job Satisfaction and Retirement Agency

In one of our own studies (Bacharach, Bamberger, Biron, & Horowitz-Rozen, 2008), we posited that preretirement job satisfaction might interact with retirement agency to affect retirees' drinking behavior. We reasoned that, in general, the more retirees viewed themselves as having been forced into retirement, the more negative and dysphoric the retirement experience would be and the greater the retirees' risk of increased alcohol consumption and problem drinking. At the same time, we expected that the relationship between retirement agency and drinking behavior would be affected by how satisfied those individuals were with their jobs while they were working. That is, it seemed likely that people who felt they had been forced to retire would react more negatively to retirement if they had been highly satisfied with their jobs than if they saw work as an unpleasant experience. Likewise, we theorized that people who had enjoyed high job satisfaction would react less negatively to retirement if they perceived it as wholly voluntary compared to those who felt retirement was forced upon them. In both cases, we reasoned that these interactions would translate into differences in modal alcohol consumption (quantity and frequency) and in drinking problems, as measured by the Drinking Problems Index (DPI, Table 1.4).

We analyzed data from 304 blue-collar workers drawn from our larger study who retired within the first 2 years after they became eligible to do so. The data used for this analysis were collected 6 months prior to retirement eligibility (time 1) and 3 years after the first interview (time 2), meaning that at time 2 respondents had been retired for at least 6 months and up to 2.5 years. At time 2, most of the 304 respondents were male (82%), white (88%), and married (84%; all the figures were similar for time 1).

We measured respondents' job satisfaction at time 1 by asking them questions such as "Would you recommend your job to a close friend or family member?" Answers were on a 5-point scale, from "not at all" to "very much so"; and there were four questions, allowing for total scores of 4 through 20. We measured retirement agency at time 2 using questions that assessed "push" versus "pull" factors (Shultz et al., 1998)—that is, the degree to which respondents felt they had been pushed to retire by various considerations, such as poor health, versus the degree to which they had responded to the pull of postretirement enticements, such as wanting to pursue other activities or spend time with a retired spouse. To avoid conceptual overlap with job satisfaction, the "push" factors were all non-job-related. Like the job satisfaction items, all the push–pull items were measured on a 5-point scale, from "not at all important" to "very important," allowing for a nuanced assessment of respondents' different motivations for retiring. Fifty participants (16%) scored within the highest quartile for "push" and the lowest quartile for "pull" factors and were operationalized as unwilling or involuntary retires. Eighty-six respondents (28%) scored in the lowest quartile for "push" and the highest for "pull" factors and were categorized as voluntary retirees. These figures are in keeping with the proportions of voluntary and involuntary retirees reported by Shultz et al. (1998).

To ensure that our analyses would capture the effects of agency and job satisfaction, we controlled for a large number of other variables that might affect drinking behavior, including sociodemographic characteristics (gender, age, education level, and so on), physical and emotional health, and negative life events (divorce, death of a family member, etc.). We also controlled for preretirement drinking behavior (necessary in order to rule out a reverse cause-and-effect relationship, e.g., the possibility that individuals who drink more are more likely to feel forced into retirement). What we found after controlling for these factors largely bore out our hypotheses. First of all, with regard to retirement volition, we found a positive association between "push" perceptions and both the quantity and frequency of drinking (though not drinking problems) and an inverse association between "pull" perceptions and both drinking frequency and drinking problems (though not quantity). In other words, it appears that respondents who felt they had been forced to retire against their wishes tended to experience retirement as a stressful life event. They began to drink more often and in larger quantities, presumably as a means of self-medicating the tension produced by the resulting sense of role loss, isolation, or lack of control. In contrast, respondents who perceived their retirement as volitional experienced retirement in positive terms. Motivated by whatever had spurred them to retire—the prospect of more leisure time or a less demanding job—they began to drink less often and were better able to manage their drinking problems.

In addition, we found support for the notion that the effect of perceived "push" and "pull" factors on the change in drinking behavior following retirement may itself be contingent on preretirement job attitudes. That is, greater job satisfaction amplified the positive association between "push" perceptions and alcohol consumption and attenuated the inverse association between "pull" perceptions and unhealthy or problematic drinking. This moderating effect of preretirement job valence, which is consistent with the implications of earlier studies on retirement, suggests that people who are most happy in their jobs are likely to fare worst in response to the stress of a retirement that is unplanned or undesired. At the same time, even when retirement is the result of personal volition, it may still be associated with a sense of loss and negative emotions, for which alcohol may serve as a coping mechanism.

Interestingly, we found no support for the notion that a sense of being pushed into retirement is associated with increases in the average quantity of alcohol consumed on any given drinking occasion. This may have to do with the way the effects of alcohol at the cellular and organ levels are altered by the physiological changes associated with aging described in chapter 1. In particular, the decline in lean tissue and water in older age means that a given amount of alcohol is distributed in a smaller volume, resulting in increased alcohol concentration with any given dose of alcohol (Dufour & Fuller, 1995; Oslin, 2000; Smith, 1995). Therefore, it may be that retirees who use alcohol to self-medicate negative emotions need not consume large quantities in order to feel the effects.

Workplace Social Networks and a History of Problem Drinking

In our 2007 report mentioned in chapter 3 (Bacharach et al., 2007), we examined whether changes in the depth (i.e., the quality) and breadth (the size and composition) of social networks affect retirement's impact on the severity of problem drinking. In this study, we took as our starting point evidence from previous work suggesting that most of the variance in drinking behavior over time can be attributed to older adults who have a baseline history of heavy or problem drinking (Atkinson et al., 1990; Liberto, Osline, & Ruskin, 1992). That is, for the vast majority of older adults who either abstain from alcohol or consume it in moderation, drinking behavior remains relatively stable into more advanced ages. This would suggest that if changes in the depth and breadth of support networks following retirement have a salient influence on drinking behavior, these effects may be most manifest among those having a baseline history of drinking problems. Recall also the finding of Brennan et al. (2010), discussed in chapter 3, that retired status had no effect on drinking trajectories once problem-drinking history was considered.

We analyzed data for 71 male retirees who met the criterion for problem drinking at the study's start, along with 236 fellow male retirees who did not meet this criterion. The criterion for problem drinking was a score of 1 or more on the DPI, based on earlier research we conducted suggesting that among older adults a DPI score as low as 1 is strongly associated with both a pattern of heavy drinking and a wide range of alcohol-related physiological problems (Bamberger, Sonnenstuhl, & Vashdi, 2006). Among the 71 problem drinkers, scores on the DPI at time 1 ranged from 1 to 18, with a mean of 3.72. All participants began receiving retirement benefits before time 2 (2 years after the first interview).

We measured breadth of social support by asking the respondents to provide the initials or first names of those adult individuals to whom they felt the closest. The number of people identified ranged from none to four at baseline, with most respondents providing three or four names. Change in breadth of support over the study period ranged from –3 (meaning that the number of close individuals fell by 3) to +2 (the number rose by 2), with 87% reporting no net change. To assess depth of support, we asked respondents how much they could rely on each of those individuals for tangible support (e.g., money or food) at times of need, on a scale of 1 to 4; these scores were then added to create a total for this variable. Values for change in the depth of support ranged from −7 to +7, with both the mean and median falling very close to 0. As in all our studies, we also collected data on a variety of control variables, including age, change in marital status, and change in health status. Finally, because drinking behaviors as well as both the breadth and depth of social support prior to retirement may be linked to occupational cultures, we also included respondents' union affiliations in our analyses (the unions represented transport workers, unskilled assembly-line workers, machinists, and so on, as described in chapter 1).

Our analyses of the relationships among the variables produced two sets of interesting findings. First, problem drinking among the 71 respondents in the problem-drinking cohort diminished overall during the 2 years between the first and second interviews, with the mean score on the DPI falling from 3.72 to 2.45; the change in scores ranged from −14 to +8. (DPI scores at the end of the 2 years ranged from 0 to 19.) In contrast, among the participants with no baseline history of drinking problems, retirement had no significant impact on the probability of a drinking problem at the end of the study. In other words, consistent with previous findings (e.g., Perreira & Sloan, 2001), we too found that the effects of retirement on drinking behavior are more robust among those with a history of problem drinking. However, our finding that retirement is associated with a net decline in the severity of drinking problems diverges from that of Perreira and Sloan (2001), who reported a lower likelihood of reduced consumption following retirement among baseline problem drinkers.

The source for these divergent findings may lie in the fact that Perreira and Sloan examined modal consumption, whereas the focus in our study was the variance in drinking problems. It is possible that among older individuals drinking problems are associated more with periodic heavy drinking than with average daily consumption. If retirees engage in fewer episodes of periodic heavy drinking, problem drinking may decline even if average daily consumption remains about the same. Alternatively, the discrepancy may lie with the difference between a sample drawn from the general population (as in Perreira and Sloan's study) and a blue-collar workforce (as in our research). If problem drinking among blue-collar workers is associated with occupationally specific permissive drinking norms, then workers who retire from those occupations should find it easier to manage and reduce their problem drinking.

This possibility leads into our second set of findings, which relate to the role of social support networks in explaining the association between retirement and the change in drinking problems. Importantly, our analyses suggested that most of the changes we measured could be attributed to shifts in the breadth of retirees' social support. Specifically, those respondents whose social networks became more consolidated over the study period saw their drinking problems drop in severity, while those whose social networks expanded experienced the opposite—that is, their drinking problems became more severe over time. However, only the former was statistically related to retirement. The findings thus show that at least a portion of the inverse association between retirement and problem drinking operates via the role of retirement in shrinking old support networks. Retirement may mean less time with work buddies—but, potentially, less contact with drinking buddies at the same time.

Unit-Level Drinking Norms and Unit-Level Stress Climate

In a more recent study (Nahum-Shani, Bamberger, Bacharach, & Doveh, 2013), we examined whether two key aspects of the work environment moderate the relationship between retirement and drinking: unit-level drinking norms and unit-level stress climate. The former reflects the degree to which the alcohol-related behavior of those in the employee's immediate work unit facilitate or support heavier consumption, while the latter involves the degree to which unit members collectively experience interpersonal and task-related stressors at work. In this study we tested for moderating effects of each of these work-unit conditions on modal alcohol consumption (quantity and frequency) in retirement and then tested for a three-way interaction between retirement and the two conditions. In point of fact, we made the analyses even more meaningful by looking not merely at work units but also at groups of "cohort peers"—those members who joined a particular work unit at around the same time. There is strong evidence that within any group or organization cohort peers tend to be closer to and more influenced by each other than by their peers who entered earlier or later and that they rely on each other for insights into what comprises normative behavior (Harrison & Carroll, 2006; Pfeffer, 1983). This study thus considers the individual and combined effects of stress and drinking norms among the group of peers who presumably had the most salient influence on participants during their working lives.

In this study, we used survey data from the preretirement interview and the first postretirement interview a year later. Five hundred and eighty-four participants from 59 work units met the two unit-level inclusion criteria (a within-unit response rate of at least 50% and a minimum of three participants from the work unit). Of these, 72 participants (12% of the sample) had retired by the second interview. Men made up 64% of the sample.

We measured unit-level stress climate by asking three questions based on a scale developed by Moos and Moos (1994): "In the past year, how much has your life been troubled by (1) a change in your line of work; (2) troubles with your boss or coworkers; or (3) a decrease in your responsibilities or hours of work," with responses given on a scale from 1 to 5. We averaged these scores for each individual and then aggregated the scores for each cohort peer group to produce a unit-level score. To measure drinking norms, we simply asked participants whether they regularly consumed alcohol; we then computed unit-level drinking norms as the proportion of cohort peers within the unit who answered "yes" to that question.

As expected, we found that, overall, alcohol consumption fell among the 72 participants who had retired by the second interview, while it remained steady among the 512 who remained in their career jobs. The interesting results related to the unit-level variables. In setting out, we expected that unit-level drinking norms would moderate the retirement–drinking relationship such that alcohol consumption would fall more steeply among retirees whose cohort peer group had maintained more permissive drinking norms (compared to norms which favored more restrained drinking). Likewise, we expected that unit-level stress climate would moderate this relationship to produce a greater drop in consumption among retirees whose work units had been characterized by greater levels of stress. Indeed, both of these expectations were confirmed for the frequency of alcohol consumption, though not for quantity. In other words, participants tended to reduce their drinking frequency once they disengaged from an environment where consuming alcohol was a form of social glue, a way to shore up friendships and reinforce a sense of belonging. Likewise, their drinking declined when they transitioned out of a more stressful work environment. These findings are in keeping with research over various age groups suggesting that social factors (i.e., drinking to fit in with social groups and perceived normative values) and coping (i.e., drinking to deal with stress) are the two most important distinct motivations for alcohol use (Cooper, 1994; Cooper, Russell, Skinner, Frone, & Mudar, 1992; Cox & Klinger, 1988).

But even more interesting findings appeared when we analyzed the three-way interaction between retirement, stress climate, and drinking norms. These results revealed that when cohort peer groups were characterized by either a highly stressful climate or permissive drinking norms alone—that is, a high-stress climate but more moderate drinking norms or permissive drinking norms but a more relaxed climate—the fall in consumption frequency following retirement was not statistically significant. A statistically significant decline was visible only when both conditions were high. Also interesting, when both conditions were low, the retirement–frequency relationship was positive, with retirees from such units consuming alcohol more frequently after retirement than prior to it. Together, these findings suggest that the salutary effects of disengagement from either a high-stress workplace or a highly permissive drinking environment, by itself, may be relatively minor if other workplace conditions did not also contribute to a higher risk of alcohol misuse prior to retirement. They also suggest that while retirement from high-risk work environments may offer relief and protection against future alcohol misuse, retirement from low-risk environments may be associated with heightened vulnerability. But as this study analyzed data only from first-year retirees, we must be careful about drawing such conclusions.

The Role of Alcohol-Related Expectations: Alcohol Expectancies, Problem Drinking, Retirement, and Aging

Our 10-year research project focuses on a population whose members, to one degree or another, all chose to work in occupations with relatively permissive drinking norms. In the study just described, we found the strongest inverse association between retirement and the frequency of alcohol use in cases where those norms were especially permissive. In Bacharach et al. (2007), we similarly found a significant decrease in problem drinking among our sample of baseline problem drinkers once they retired.

There are theoretical reasons to postulate that where alcohol misuse is associated with permissive drinking norms, retirees should find it easier to reduce their consumption and manage their problem drinking. The reasoning involves people's expectations about how alcohol will affect their behavior, moods, and emotions—what researchers call "alcohol expectancies" (Leigh & Stacy, 2004). Research has consistently shown that positive alcohol expectancies play a significant role in explaining the initiation and maintenance of drinking behaviors across a wide variety of demographic subgroups, including older adults (Goldman, 1994; Leigh & Stacy, 2004). Moreover, there is strong and consistent evidence that alcohol expectancies moderate the relationship between stress and drinking behaviors (e.g., Cooper et al., 1992; Johnson & Gurin, 1994).

In one of our studies (Bacharach, Bamberger, Sonnenstuhl, & Vashdi, 2008a), we examined whether alcohol expectancies moderate the relationship between retirement and drinking behavior. We took as our starting point the notion that for individuals in occupations characterized by permissive drinking norms, such as those represented in our sample, positive associations between drinking and outcomes are likely to be framed around the workplace. Workers may drink to maintain a sense of camaraderie and occupational community, along with relief from work-based stressors. Cognitive psychology (and, in particular, the information processing perspective) suggests that the degree to which alcohol expectancies influence actual drinking behavior depends on whether expectancy-relevant information—associations between context, drinking behavior, and expected outcomes—is activated on exposure to particular stimuli. If this is true, then expectancies associated with the work context—with work-based camaraderie and relief from work-based stressors—might diminish in importance (or, more accurately, simply not be activated) following retirement, when that work context is no longer relevant.

Our data for this analysis came from 501 respondents who participated in the first five waves of our larger study—that is, from 6 months before they became eligible for retirement (time 1) to 4 years later (time 5). The sociodemographics of the larger sample from which the 501 were drawn remained roughly the same over the study period (for time 1 and time 5, respectively, 69% and 67% were men, 76% and 77% were married, and 80% and 83% were white). Forty percent of the respondents remained in the active workforce at time 5, most in their original jobs, while the other 60% had taken retirement benefits.

We measured positive alcohol expectancies at time 4 and time 5 only, using an instrument developed by Leigh and Stacy (1993). This instrument asks respondents to report how drinking would affect them or (for abstainers) how they think drinking would affect them in relation to a list of 17 items (see Table 4.1). The respondents were asked to rate each item on a 5-point scale, from "very unlikely" to "certain." Based on these scores, we categorized positive alcohol expectancies as low, medium, or high. Because the expectancies data did not differ between time 4 and time 5 and because previous studies have found that such expectancies are stable over time (Fromme, Stroot, & Kaplan, 1993; Kline, 1996; Werner, Walker, & Greene, 1995), we used the time 5 expectancy scores for all our analyses.

Before analyzing the data on retirement, we tested for a relationship between alcohol expectancies, problem drinking, and aging. Unsurprisingly, with reference to the first time point, we found that predicted drinking problems were relatively high for respondents with high positive alcohol

Table 4.1. POSITIVE ALCOHOL EXPECTANCIES QUESTIONNAIRE

Here is a list of some effects or consequences that some people experience after drinking alcohol. How likely is it that these things happen to YOU when you drink alcohol? Please indicate how drinking alcohol would affect you. If you do not drink at all, you can indicate what you think would happen if you DID drink alcohol. "When I drink alcohol it is very unlikely, unlikely, very likely, or certain to happen that..."

I am more accepted socially.

I am more outgoing.

It is easier for me to socialize.

I am able to talk more freely.

I am friendlier.

I feel more social.

I enjoy the buzz.

I feel happy.

I have a good time.

It is fun.

I feel pleasant physical effects.

I feel good.

It takes away my negative moods and feelings.

I feel less stressed.

I am able to take my mind off my problems.

I find that I can be closer to my spouse/partner.

I am more relaxed with my spouse/partner.

Note. Adapted from Leigh, B. C., & Stacy, A. W. (1993). Alcohol outcome expectancies: Scale construction and predictive utility in higher order confirmatory models. *Psychological Assessment, 5,* 216–229.

expectancies, moderate for those with medium expectancies, and low for those with low expectancies. Importantly, though, for the high-expectancies group, predicted drinking problems tended to increase over the 5 years of the study. For the medium-expectancies group the line predicting drinking problems was relatively stable, and for the low-expectancies group it fell with time. In other words, it appears that individuals who have very high expectations about how alcohol will make them feel and what will happen to them when they drink tend to develop more drinking problems as they age, while for people whose expectations are less positive, the risk of developing drinking problems stays the same or even falls with aging. These effects are shown in Figure 4.2.

The next step was to test whether retirement would attenuate the positive association between aging and problem drinking as a function of positive alcohol expectancies. For this analysis, we divided the participants into those who were still in the active workforce and those who had retired by time 2—that is, the first year after all participants became eligible for

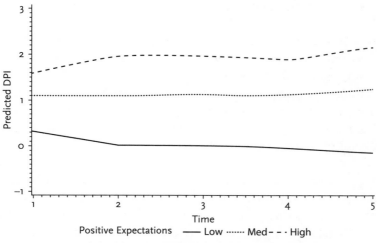

Positive Expectations   —— Low ······· Med- - · High

*Low = 1 SD below the mean positive alcohol expectancy [PAE] score, medium = mean PAE score, and high = 1 SD above the mean PAE score.

Figure 4.2:
The Moderating Effects of Positive Alcohol Expectancies* on the Relationship Between Aging and Predicted Drinking Problems Among Mature Adults.
DPI = Drinking Problems Index.
Reprinted with permission from Bacharach, S., Bamberger, P., Sonnenstuhl, W., & Vashdi, D. (2008a). Aging and drinking problems among mature adults: The moderating effects of positive alcohol expectancies and workforce disengagement. *Journal of Studies on Alcohol and Drugs, 69*(1), 151–159.

retirement. After we eliminated the 72 respondents who had taken retirement benefits but were working in some form of bridge employment, those who had fully retired numbered 276 respondents and those still working numbered 153. Among the latter, we found a pattern similar to that which had emerged when we looked at the full sample, meaning that high alcohol expectancies seemed to amplify the relationship between aging and problem drinking, while low alcohol expectancies seemed to attenuate that relationship. On the other hand, for those who had left the workforce, alcohol expectancies had no significant impact on this relationship, suggesting that these expectancies were no longer relevant in retirees' day-to-day lives.

Overall, the findings from this study suggest that for older adults in occupations characterized by highly permissive drinking norms, the workplace serves as an important referent for shaping expectations about alcohol. Once these individuals retire, the relevance and salience of those expectations diminish. Even if people are subject to stress in retirement, the different context of that stress means that alcohol-related expectancies developed in the workplace are no longer activated.

SUMMARY AND CONCLUSION

The studies reported in this chapter suggest a number of preliminary conclusions about how aspects of work life may interact with other variables, including individual attributes and personal history, to affect retirees' risk of unhealthy or problem drinking. For example, leaving work-based social networks seems to serve as a protective factor, particularly if these work-based networks are characterized by highly permissive drinking norms and/or if the individuals involved enter retirement life already burdened with drinking problems. Leaving a highly stressful work environment appears also to be a protective factor. However, there is also evidence that the effects of workplace stress can linger into retirement, especially for women. Such lingering workplace stress, along with a combination of high job satisfaction and low retirement volition, seem to raise the likelihood that people will drink more than they should following retirement, at least in the early period (up to a few years).

In the next chapter we will enlarge this picture by looking at studies that focus on how conditions and relationships in retirement may affect older adults' drinking behavior.

CHAPTER 5

How Conditions and Relationships in Retirement Influence Drinking in Retirement

As we've seen, the earliest stages of retirement can be characterized as a transition out of the work-based conditions and social networks that may alternatively promote or deter risky patterns of alcohol use. As time passes, though, the conditions and relationships that were important during one's working life begin to lose their salience. They pass into the realm of memory and experience, retaining their significance in shaping people's sense of self and their own life history but giving way to more present concerns in day-to-day life.

In this chapter, we will consider how some of these more present concerns might help shape people's drinking behavior as they transition into retirement. To put this chapter into the context of Wang's (2007) suggested trajectories, our interest here is no longer the very beginning of the time line, as in chapter 4, nor yet the long period where the three paths move—first slowly, then more rapidly—toward convergence. Our focus here remains roughly within the first third of Figure 5.1, where many retirees face new challenges in the adjustment to retired life. After that, as the disengagement from work recedes further into the past, it, too, loses its salience. That is, for longtime retirees, retirement (like work) is no longer an emotional or psychological force with the power to help shape behavior but simply part of one's life history, an element in the backdrop to old age.

Retirees may face several sets of challenges during this period. First, for some, there is the challenge of having to make do with less. We have already

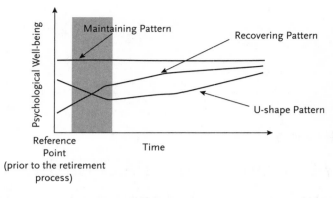

Figure 5.1:
Patterns of Change in Psychological Well-Being During the Retirement Transition and Adjustment Process. The Highlighted Area Shows the Period of Interest in This Chapter.
Source: Wang, M. (2007). Profiling retirees in the retirement transition and adjustment process: Examining the longitudinal change patterns of retirees' psychological well-being. *Journal of Applied Psychology, 92*(2), p. 457.

discussed the potential strains inherent in replacing a salary or career income with a fixed or reduced income from pensions and other retirement benefits (such as Social Security payments). Social and interpersonal relationships produce a second set of challenges. Even after retirees have adjusted to making their non-work-related roles (spouse, parent of older children, and so on) more central in their lives, their interpersonal relationships are likely to involve conflicts, compromise, and readjustments. A third set of challenges falls in the realm of health and wellness. While failing health is in the natural course of things a consequence of aging and not associated with retirement per se, health concerns (for oneself or loved ones) may constrain people's choices and shape their experience of retired life. In addition, any of these areas may interact with any of the others to heighten their impact. For instance, financial constraints may become even more salient for retirees who foresee that they or their spouse will need expensive, long-term care. Similarly, marital stress may intensify as couples adjust to getting by on less income.

As should be clear by now, the research that might help us clarify how these challenges interact with personal characteristics and life history to produce particular alcohol-related outcomes is still very young and, as a result, the literature is extremely sparse. Indeed, to have produced a published study relating to this stage in the retirement process, a longitudinal project would have to be at least 10 years old at the time of this writing. As far as we know, our own research project, begun in 2000–2001, is one of the few thus far to have examined how individual factors interact with stressors characteristic of the early-middle stage of the retirement adjustment process to help shape alcohol use. We will discuss our research later on in this chapter.

STRESS, RESOURCES, AND DRINKING IN LATER LIFE: INSIGHTS FROM THE STANFORD STUDY

In the absence of studies dealing specifically with the nexus of retirement, individual factors, and drinking, we must draw insights from other sources. Some interesting findings in this regard have come from a 20-year longitudinal study led by Penny Brennan, Rudolf Moos, and Kathleen Schutte of Stanford University. These researchers drew their initial sample from individuals aged 55 to 65 recruited from the databases of two large outpatient health care facilities. All those selected for the study either consumed alcohol at least once a week or had had drinking problems in the recent past; lifetime abstainers and very light drinkers were excluded. At each stage of the research, participants filled out detailed questionnaires concerning life stressors, social resources, coping responses, drinking behavior, and psychosocial well-being. The initial data were gathered in 1986–1988 from 1,884 respondents born between 1921 and 1933, with follow-up surveys at various points over the next two decades. Over the 20 years of the study, slightly more than half the initial respondents died, while others were lost to attrition; 719 respondents were surveyed at the close of the project in 2006–2008.

The first study based on this long-term project was a cross-sectional comparison between problem drinkers and drinkers who did not have alcohol-related problems. Brennan and Moos (1990) compared relationships among various factors—chronic stressors, acute negative life events, and social resources—between the two groups. They also explored how life stressors and social resources might affect drinkers on four measures: alcohol consumption (frequency and quantity), drinking problems, depression, and self-confidence. Unfortunately for our purposes, the authors did not report data for retirement specifically. However, as the respondents were all aged 65 or under at the study's start, it is safe to assume that most were either still working or in the early stages of the retirement transition when they were first surveyed.

The researchers classified as problem drinkers participants who responded positively to two or more items on the Drinking Problems Index (DPI, see Table 1.4). Non–problem drinkers were defined to exclude former problem drinkers and participants who scored positive for only one item on the DPI. Based on these criteria, the sample for this study included 501

problem drinkers (387 men and 114 women) and 609 non–problem drinkers (299 men and 310 women). Quantity was measured in two ways: typical consumption of beer, wine, and hard liquor on days when drinking
occurred over the last month and the largest amount of each type of alcohol consumed in 1 day over the last month. Frequency was assessed as
the number of times per week that the typical and largest quantities were
consumed.

An important feature of this study is its detailed differentiation among
various types of stressors. The researchers differentiated between acute,
short-term negative life events and chronic, long-term stressors and, further, between various domains of stressors. Acute stressors were measured
through a list of 86 discrete events (e.g., having a home burglarized, being
demoted at work, or the death of a spouse). Potential chronic stressors
were measured in a number of specific domains, including physical health,
the home and neighborhood, financial problems, work-related stress, and
different types of interpersonal relationships (spouse, children, extended
family, and friends). Social resources were assessed in terms of financial
resources (total annual family income), work resources (challenges, inde-
pendence, and support at work), and interpersonal resources (spouse, children, extended family, and friends).

As expected, problem drinkers reported experiencing more stressors,
both acute and chronic, and fewer social resources than non–problem
drinkers. In general, male respondents reported more financial problems,
more stressful friendships, and less support from children, extended family, and friends, while female respondents reported more negative life
events, more ongoing stress related to their spouse and extended family,
and less support from their spouses. These disparities were especially pro-
nounced among the problem drinkers. Overall, the women in the sample
drank less and had fewer drinking problems than the men, even though
they were also more depressed. Marriage, in general, seemed to protect
against both problem drinking and depression for both sexes. Negative life
events (i.e., acute stressors) explained a small but statistically significant
amount of the variance in drinking problems and depression, though not
modal consumption, while chronic stressors were significantly associated
with problem drinking and consumption as well as depression.

As this study was cross-sectional in nature, the authors could draw no
conclusions about the direction of causality in most of the relationships
identified. Indeed, they point out that many of the relationships they found
are likely to reflect the effects of drinking on other factors rather than the
reverse or may even be reciprocal. For instance, among problem drinkers,
men were more likely to report chronic stress involving friends. Because

men with drinking problems tend to drink in groups (unlike women with drinking problems, who are more likely to drink alone; Cronkite & Moos, 1984), their drinking may offer more opportunities for interpersonal conflict. Male problem drinkers were also more likely than their female counterparts to report chronic financial hardship. Perhaps some of these men drank to mitigate the strain of dealing with money problems, or perhaps the cost of maintaining a drinking habit contributed to those financial concerns. Meanwhile, women with drinking problems reported receiving more support from children, extended family, and friends compared to male problem drinkers but less support from their spouse. At the same time, female problem drinkers reported more chronic stressors involving spouses and extended family members. These findings could suggest that at least some women turn to alcohol to alleviate strains arising from marital and family conflicts (perhaps even including problem drinking on the part of their husbands). On the other hand, women with drinking problems may fail to fulfill socially prescribed domestic roles, which in turn may trigger conflicts within the family (Brennan & Moos, 1990, p. 498).

The respondents who did not have drinking problems resembled the problem drinkers in most of the relationships between stressors, resources, and outcomes. However, they differed in a few key points. For instance, among the non–problem drinkers, those who were married tended to drink more than their single counterparts. The authors posit that non–problem drinkers tend to drink mainly in social contexts and that married people are more likely to drink during meals and to attend social occasions involving alcohol. Meanwhile, non–problem drinkers who reported more home/neighborhood and financial stressors tended to consume less alcohol—most likely, the authors suggest, because financial difficulties prompted them to cut back on alcohol purchases and limit their participation in social and leisure activities that are likely to involve drinking (e.g., parties and vacations; Brennan & Moos, 1990, p. 499).

Drinking in the Context of Retirement Adjustment: Looking Deeper

In general, Brennan and Moos's (1990) study offers a number of insights that can guide our thinking as we consider the potential contribution of retirement to drinking behavior over the medium term. First, there is a strong link between problem drinking and chronic stress, especially in certain domains, such as interpersonal conflict and financial hardship, though the direction of causality is not always clear. For instance, a good marriage seems to be protective against problem drinking, though it may simply be that problem drinking is bad for marriage. Second, financial stress seems to protect against excessive alcohol consumption for people who have never had drinking problems, but it may be less protective or even detrimental for those who do. Third, chronic stress is more important in terms of drinking outcomes than acute negative life events, whose effects seem to be more short-lived.

In a later report (Brennan et al., 1999), the Stanford researchers examined reciprocal relationships between stressors and drinking behavior and the moderating role of gender over the first 4 years of their study. In this report, the authors looked particularly at four groups of stressors—negative life events (acute stressors) and chronic stressors in three domains: health, finances, and marriage. Data were collected from three time periods (the initial assessment, 1 year later, and 3 years after that), and the final sample for this study comprised 1,562 individuals, of whom 621 were women and 941 were men. Again, the authors did not report data on retirement rates among their sample. Given that the respondents were 59 to 69 years old at the study's end, it is likely that a fair number were retired at that point but had not necessarily been so for long. Still, as before, we can draw on this study for insights that may be applicable to the questions we have posed in this chapter.

The findings of Brennan et al. (1999) join evidence from our own work and other studies (Bacharach, Bamberger, Biron, & Horowitz-Rozen, 2008; Frone, 2013) in suggesting that among older adults problem drinking can exist independently of increased modal alcohol consumption. The authors found no sign that heightened stressors of any sort significantly predicted greater modal alcohol consumption. Indeed, having more initial health stressors (among women) and more initial financial stressors (among men) predicted reductions in the quantity and frequency of consumption. However, greater levels of initial stressors did predict more drinking problems, a finding the authors explain by suggesting that greater stress may make people more belligerent when they drink or may enhance their sensitivity to the effects of alcohol (Brennan et al., 1999, p. 747). Interestingly, the moderating role of gender in this regard differed from what we would expect based on Brennan and Moos's (1990) study. Greater financial stress (along with a greater number of negative life events) at the 1-year survey predicted more drinking problems at the 4-year follow-up for women but not for men. Meanwhile, more spouse-related stressors at baseline predicted more drinking problems 1 year later for men but not for women.

For both men and women, there was also evidence for a causal link in the other direction: Problem drinking at baseline predicted more financial and spouse-related stress later in the study. However, more frequent drinking at baseline was associated with reductions in stressors of various types: health stressors, financial stressors, and negative life events for women and health problems for men. The authors interpret these findings to mean that participants who drank more frequently (but not problematically) at baseline were doing so in a context of socializing and engagement with family and friends, behavior that foreshadows better subsequent well-being and health outcomes. In fact, they suggest that there may be a "benign feedback cycle in which moderate alcohol consumption and stressors tend to reduce each other" (Brennan et al., 1999, p. 748).

More recent reports by the Stanford group extend and add to these findings. For instance, in Moos, Brennan, et al. (2010), the authors analyzed data collected at baseline and at the 10- and 20-year follow-ups to examine relationships between social and financial resources and high-risk alcohol consumption in later life. Extending their previous findings on financial resources, they found that respondents who were more financially comfortable at baseline and 10 years later were more likely to report heavy drinking in subsequent surveys. This study also found a strong influence of social selection—that is, the idea that people who drink heavily tend to choose friends or partners who approve of heavier drinking. While there is abundant evidence that this is true for younger and middle-aged adults (Bullers, Cooper, & Russell, 2001; Preston & Goodfellow, 2006), Moos, Brennan, et al. (2010) show that it is so for older adults as well.

In another study (Brennan, Schutte, SooHoo, & Moos, 2011), the Stanford researchers explored the relationship between painful medical conditions and drinking behavior. Using data collected over the study's first 10 years, they addressed the question of whether pain experienced by individuals in late middle age influences their current or subsequent use of alcohol and whether personal attributes or life context factors moderate any such relationship. To assess pain, the researchers used five items from the health-related subscale of their survey, in which respondents were asked whether they suffered from back pain, chest pain, headache, stomach pain, or joint pain. The analyses showed that at baseline individuals who reported having more of these painful medical conditions consumed alcohol less frequently but had more drinking problems than their counterparts with fewer painful conditions. The relationship between the number of painful conditions and reduced alcohol consumption was stronger for women than for men, while that between painful conditions and more drinking problems was stronger for men than for women. Having more interpersonal resources was also linked to an inverse relationship between painful conditions and drinking frequency. As for the question of how pain might impact drinking behavior over time, the number of painful conditions at baseline had, by itself, no impact on respondents' drinking over 10 years, but being older and having more interpersonal resources made it more likely that painful medical conditions at baseline would predict a decline in both the frequency of alcohol consumption and drinking problems.

Brennan et al. (2011) draw several conclusions from their findings. For instance, they argue that the negative concurrent relationship between painful medical conditions and drinking frequency means that respondents did not use alcohol to self-medicate their pain. Rather, they suggest, the pain sufferers may have limited their drinking in order to avoid adverse medical consequences, such as those potentially arising from alcohol–painkiller interactions. Alternatively, their less frequent drinking may simply mean that these individuals were participating less in activities and social events where alcohol is commonly served. Meanwhile, the positive concurrent relationship between painful medical conditions and drinking problems raises, again, interesting questions about the causal link between the two. Does pain exacerbate the negative consequences of drinking—for instance, by intensifying cravings for alcohol, aggravating alcohol-related social friction, or increasing the likelihood of falls? Or does a lifestyle that includes substance abuse increase the risk of painful illnesses and injuries? The absence of a direct effect of painful medical conditions on drinking over the subsequent 10 years testifies, according to the authors, against a causal link from pain to problem drinking (rather than the other way around). However, as the authors point out, their definition of pain is limited and fails to take into account more specific (and subjective) characteristics such as the pain's severity, duration, or chronicity. Future explorations of pain and drinking might thus reveal more nuanced influences and relationships.

As in the Stanford group's other studies, Brennan et al. (2011) did not include retirement as a variable in their analyses. But the questions they ask are important in the retirement context. In the natural course of life, retirement is likely to coincide with the onset or worsening of age-related conditions that involve pain (e.g., osteoarthritis, rheumatoid arthritis, degenerative disc disease, carpal tunnel syndrome, or heartburn and indigestion). Some people retire because their pain prevents them from working, especially individuals in physically demanding jobs (we discussed this briefly in chapter 4 in the context of retirement volition). Yet for an increasing number of older adults, whose retirement benefits fail to meet their day-to-day needs, retirement means only partial withdrawal from the workforce, which may in turn mean having to work despite physical pain.

What this implies for the interaction between retirement, bridge employment, pain, and drinking remains to be seen.

Stress and Retirement: Further Insights from the Stanford Study

The Stanford team included retirement as a variable in one study: Brennan et al. (2010), which we discussed in chapter 3. This study examined whether retired status affects older adults' 10-year drinking trajectories and whether other factors—age, gender, income, health, and problem-drinker status—account for or moderate this effect. The data for this analysis came from 595 participants, of whom 443 were fully retired and 152 fully employed throughout the study—that is, at baseline and over the subsequent 10 years. In other words, Brennan et al. did not explore how individuals' drinking patterns change as a result of the adjustments that accompany the shift from work to retirement but, rather, considered whether retired status per se can predict drinking patterns when other variables are taken into account. (The potential confounding or moderating variables, including income and health, were also all measured for this study only at baseline.)

As we described in chapter 3, Brennan et al. (2010) found that alcohol consumption declined over the study period for all participants and that retired status predicted a somewhat steeper decline. Yet the authors also found that this effect disappeared once the other variables were added to the model. Poorer health at baseline was associated with smaller quantities of alcohol consumed and with a steeper decline in drinking frequency than retired status alone. Similarly, having lower baseline income was associated with less frequent drinking initially and a faster rate of decline in both quantity and frequency. Past and present drinking problems also were more important than retired status in predicting changes in how much and how often participants drank. The authors did not test for a moderating effect of gender on these relationships.

While these findings seem to suggest that retirement, by itself, is a moderately protective factor for alcohol use, this study points to ways in which research might elicit a more nuanced picture. For instance, as we saw earlier, the authors argue that lower income is associated with lower quantity and frequency of drinking because financial constraints are likely to limit alcohol purchases as well as participation in social activities that involve alcohol (Brennan et al., 2010, p. 167). Yet, because the study treated retired status as a fixed state, it could not examine whether retirement itself might be partly responsible for some partici-pants' lower incomes.

STRESSORS IN RETIREMENT AND DRINKING: THE CRITICAL ROLE OF SLEEP

Two important questions left open by the Stanford researchers involve when and how key stressors experienced during the adjustment to retire-ment might lead to changes in older adults' drinking patterns. In our study (Belogolovsky, Bamberger, & Bacharach, 2012), we focused on two of the stressors studied by the Stanford group—financial and marital stressors—but considered them specifically in the context of retirement. That is, we focused on two stressors highlighted by the literature as highly salient for a large number of retirees and their role in influencing shifts in drinking patterns as older people adjust to retirement. Moreover, based on quali-tative data from the interviews and focus groups we conducted, we also introduced a new candidate as a potential mediator of (i.e., mechanism explaining) the stress–drinking relationship: poor-quality sleep. Following comments from some of the retirees we interviewed, we decided to inves-tigate whether at least some people who drink too much during retirement do so, at least in part, to self-medicate sleeping problems.

Both theoretical research and universal human experience testify that stress often gives rise to sleep-related problems—difficulty falling asleep or staying asleep, disturbed or restless sleep, or waking earlier than desired. The comments of several of those participating in our prestudy focus group lent support to this idea that stressors may generate or exacerbate sleep-related problems, with some older adults turning to alcohol or other substances as a means to self-medicate such a problem. For instance, Ken, a former auditor and assembly-line worker in the automotive industry, relied on alcohol during his working life to help him sleep. Ken often worked 12-hour days, from 3:00 a.m. to 3:00 p.m. He drank when he got off work, "pound[ing] down 8–10 beers in 2–3 hours." Then, he would drink whiskey at night: "That helped me to sleep, too." One of Ken's fellow assembly-line workers commented that "working nights over a period of time, you never really sleep properly" and that his sleep problems played an important role in leading him to finally retire. Carl, a tool and die maker from another manufacturing plant, complained that, 28 days postretirement, he was "still having trouble sleeping through the night."

The male retirees we interviewed were not alone in reporting sleep-related problems. Many of the women we interviewed—flight attendants in particular—noted being affected by sleep-related problems while working, with these problems continuing into retirement. One explained that such problems "come with the territory, jet lag and all." Another, who said she had trouble staying asleep, blamed concerns from when she was still flying that she would not wake up on time. A third linked her current sleep-related problems to menopause. A fourth commented that she avoided sleep problems by simply continuing to do what she had done on the job—take a combination of prescription sleeping pills: "One relaxes my muscles and the other helps me fall asleep."

Financial and Marital Stress in Relation to Retirement and Drinking

Of all the forms of stress that might arise in relation to the adjustment to retirement, financial and marital stressors are among the most important in terms of how they might contribute to poor health outcomes—including risky, unhealthy, or problematic drinking—in vulnerable people. As we have described, financial stressors may arise when income from retirement sources (such as pensions or Social Security benefits) fails to match income previously earned on the job (Beehr, 1986; Wang, 2007; Wang, Zhan, Liu, & Shultz, 2008). Indeed, research suggests that economic strains can trigger or worsen mood disturbances even if these strains are anticipated, especially in cases where people must liquidate assets or service debt on a fixed or reduced income (Dew & Yorgason, 2010). Similarly, retirement may precipitate or intensify marital stress as couples adjust to new roles at home or reduced income levels (Shultz et al., 1998; Szinovacz, 2003).

There is evidence from the unemployment literature that economic hardship and marital conflict are among a handful of stressors that are responsible for most of the adverse mental health consequences associated with workforce disengagement (Kessler, Turner, & House, 1988; Lin & Leung, 2010; McKee-Ryan, Song, Wanberg, & Kinicki, 2005; Price, Choi, & Vinokur, 2002). Yet, to date, we have little understanding of how these stressors affect specific mental health outcomes such as alcohol misuse and, in particular, how they mediate this relationship among individuals disengaging from the workforce on a more permanent basis—namely, retirees.

Adding in Sleep and Gender

In our study (Belogolovsky et al., 2012), we examined the extent to which financial and marital stressors in retirement may be linked to the onset or exacerbation of alcohol misuse among older adults. We also sought to understand how such stressors may affect alcohol misuse among older adults. We posited that retirees might use alcohol not only to cope directly with such stressors but also to help manage the sleep-related problems that arise as a secondary effect of stress. We also posited that gender would serve as a key boundary condition, moderating both the impact of such stressors on sleep-related problems and the impact of sleep-related problems on alcohol misuse.

From a theoretical perspective, our reasoning in this study conforms only in part to Conger's (1956) tension reduction hypothesis—that is, the idea that people may use alcohol to mitigate the strain generated by exposure to stressors (we described this hypothesis in chapter 2). More deeply, it is grounded in Hobfoll's (1988, 1989) conservation of resources theory. In his resource ecology approach, Hobfoll conceptualized stress in terms of the drain on psychological resources—for example, self-esteem, self-sufficiency, or a sense of control—as people cope or attempt to cope with threats to key personal resources, such as financial resources or supportive relationships. As psychological resources become depleted, individuals often reject resource-costly, problem-focused coping strategies in favor of maladaptive strategies which seem to conserve resources in the short run but can result over time in the emergence of *loss spirals*—a pattern of increasingly more rapid depletion of the resources needed to offset stress and improve well-being. Such maladaptive strategies may include alcohol misuse.

This perspective suggests both a direct and an indirect effect of financial and marital stressors on alcohol misuse. That is, there is reason to believe that at least some of the effect of such stressors on alcohol misuse may be indirect, with people turning to alcohol to mitigate the physiological consequences of strain, such as sleep-related problems. Sleep disorders are a common manifestation of resource drain and depletion (Söderström, Ekstedt, Åkerstedt, Nilsson, & Axelsson, 2004; Vela-Bueno et al., 2008). As most people know from experience, the physical and psychological consequences of strain and anxiety (racing thoughts, a rapid heart rate) can make it hard to fall asleep or to get a good night's rest. Over time, these patterns can become self-reinforcing, with the inability to fall asleep itself becoming a source of further anxiety. Physiologically, stress interferes with the hypothalamic–pituitary–adrenal (HPA) axis (Melamed, Shirom, Toker, Berliner, & Shapira, 2006). The HPA axis is a crucial part of the neuroendocrine system that helps regulate digestion, mood and emotion, energy expenditure and storage, sexuality, and the immune system through a complex set of feedback interactions with other neurobiological systems, including the sleep–wake cycle.

Research suggests that people experiencing sleep problems often employ alcohol as a means of self-medication, based on the belief that alcohol will help them relax and fall asleep. Indeed, in one national poll, more than 30% of American adults with persistent insomnia reported using alcohol in such a manner (Ancoli-Israel & Roth, 1999). Studies also suggest that older people are particularly likely to self-medicate sleep problems through alcohol (Johnson, 1997; Roth, 2005).

Accordingly, in our study we assessed the degree to which sleep-related problems mediate the effect of financial and marital stressors on retiree alcohol misuse. Further, we examined whether these relationships and interactions may differ for men and women. Here, we considered both (1) the likelihood that retirement-related stressors would lead to sleep problems and (2) the likelihood that such sleep problems would lead to alcohol misuse. Regarding the former, numerous epidemiological studies since the 1970s have found a higher prevalence of sleep-related problems among women, particularly older women, than among men (e.g., Quan et al., 2005). Further, there is evidence that environmental stressors may take a greater toll on women's sleep than on men's (Kushnir & Melamed, 1992). While the mechanisms underlying this heightened sensitivity remain unclear—possibilities include biological differences in sex steroids and hormone-related changes following menopause (e.g., Landis & Moe, 2004; Lee-Chiong, 2006)—it seemed almost certain that we would find that women are more vulnerable than men to developing sleep problems in reaction to retirement-related stress.

Regarding the link between sleep problems and alcohol misuse, the evidence is equally strong that men are more likely than women to deal with sleep-related problems by drinking. Again, the evidence comes from both epidemiological studies and research exploring psychological processes. For instance, a recent study of over 20,000 Finnish adults found that men who experience sleep problems are nearly five times more likely to engage in periodic heavy drinking than women experiencing such problems (Hublin, Partinen, Koskenvuo, & Kaprio, 2007). Meanwhile, several studies suggest that while the pharmacological effects of alcohol may be stress-reducing for both men and women, the cognitive impact is different, with women expecting less relaxation after drinking than men (e.g., Rohsenow, 1983). Other research has found that women are more likely to deal with sleep problems by using tranquilizers or sleeping pills (Lex, 1991), a solution that has its own problems but which is not the focus of the current volume.

Taken together, these various lines of reasoning suggest that financial and marital stressors serve as primary antecedents of shifts in retiree alcohol misuse but that their effects are mediated by the impact of such

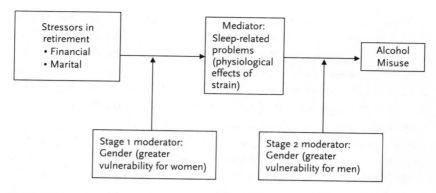

Figure 5.2:
How and For Whom Stressors in Retirement May Link to Alcohol Misuse.
Source: Belogolovsky, E., Bamberger, P., & Bacharach, S. (2012). Stressors and retiree alcohol misuse: The mediating effects of sleep problems and the moderating effects of gender. *Human Relations, 65*, 705–728.

stressors on sleep-related problems and moderated by gender. Formally, we proposed a moderated mediation model similar to those described in chapter 2 (Figure 5.2).

We tested this model on the basis of three waves of data from our longitudinal study, collected respectively at 6 years, 7.5 years, and 9.5 years after the initial contact (6 months prior to respondents becoming eligible for retirement). All the participants in this study had opted to fully retire (i.e., to completely withdraw from the workforce) prior to the first wave in late 2006, meaning that by the third wave of data collection in 2010 all participants had been retired for nearly 4 years at minimum and possibly as long as 9 years. Further, as hospitalization would likely have an effect on drinking, we excluded retirees who had been hospitalized in the year prior to the first wave of data collection. The 292 participants in the final sample included 221 male and 71 female retirees.

For this study, we assessed alcohol misuse on the basis of the DPI at the first and third waves of data collection. We measured financial and marital stressors at the first wave. For the former, we asked participants a series of questions about their ability to afford food, medical care, and other items, to be answered on a 5-point scale from "never" to "often" (e.g., "How often in the past year did you not have enough money to afford the kind of food you or your family should have?"). For the latter, we asked two questions, also answered on a 5-point scale (from "never" to "several times a day"): "How often do you and your partner get on each others' nerves?" and "How often do you and your partner quarrel?" Sleep-related problems were measured at the second wave of data collection via the widely used Pittsburgh Sleep Quality Index (Buysse, Reynolds, Monk, Berman, & Kupfer, 1989). This self-administered questionnaire assesses quality of sleep during the previous month and includes 19 items covering seven areas of interest, including subjective sleep quality, sleep duration and disturbance, and daytime dysfunction. Each area is scored from 0 to 3, yielding a global score of 0 to 21 (higher scores mean greater sleep-related problems). Finally, we also controlled for a number of variables, including education, years since retirement, physical health, and alcohol misuse prior to retirement.

The initial results only partially bore out our hypotheses. In general, for the sample as a whole, financial stressors, but not marital stressors, were positively related to alcohol misuse 3.5 years later. Both financial and marital stressors were positively related to sleep problems at the second wave of data collection. However, sleep-related problems at the second wave were not significantly related to alcohol misuse at the third, meaning that poor sleep quality, in general, does not appear to mediate the relationship between stressors in retirement and alcohol misuse. This was not entirely surprising to us, however, as we anticipated that the link between sleep-related problems and alcohol misuse would be gender-contingent and would not be generalizable across both men and women.

Indeed, the analyses for the model incorporating gender paint a fuller and more nuanced picture. First, the impact of financial (though not marital) stress on sleep-related problems was significantly moderated by gender, with women—as we anticipated—far more likely to suffer from poor sleep when confronted with financial worries. Second, and more important for our model, gender significantly moderated the impact of sleep-related problems on alcohol misuse, with men who reported sleeping poorly far more likely than other men to end up with drinking problems. Moreover, further analyses showed that the indirect effects of sleep problems explained roughly half the total effect of financial stressors on male retirees' alcohol misuse. For marital stressors that figure was two-thirds, meaning that many of the men in shaky marriages who misused alcohol did so largely in order to deal with sleep problems attributable to marital strain.

In short, our findings showed that two key stressors (financial and marital) experienced in retirement are likely to trigger or aggravate alcohol misuse among male retirees and that, at least in part, these men use alcohol in order to cope with a secondary effect of those stressors—namely, sleep-related problems. Equally, while only a relatively small number of men who face financial and marital stress in retirement suffer from poor sleep as a result, those who do are at greater risk of turning to alcohol as a solution.

Our findings suggest two important implications for policy and practice. First, they highlight the need to recognize financial and marital stressors in retirement as potential risk factors for retirees' well-being, especially among men. Second, they underscore the key role potentially played by sleep-related problems as mediating the effects of financial stressors in retirement on male retirees' well-being.

SUMMARY AND CONCLUSION

The research described in this chapter reinforces the point we have been making throughout this book, that it is not retirement per se that necessarily drives shifts in drinking patterns but conditions and experiences prior to and during retirement. More specifically, the research highlights several key risk factors in retirement of which older adults, employers, health care professionals, and policy makers should be mindful, including financial and marital strain, acute stressors, and physical pain. The research also points out that the impact of these factors on drinking is not necessarily straightforward. Rather, the effects may be limited to certain subgroups (such as men) and may operate through a variety of intermediary factors (such as sleep-related problems).

Speaking practically, all of the studies reviewed in this chapter suggest a need to go beyond simply helping older adults plan for and adjust to retirement so as to mitigate the stresses associated with it. Rather, they suggest that primary care physicians and other care professionals who treat retirees should be sensitive to the potential implications of stress on other variables, such as the quality of sleep, and should be ready to offer more effective and less risky means to deal with them. The findings also suggest the value of extending employee assistance services to retirees as a means to facilitate early intervention, an issue we will return to in chapter 7.

CHAPTER 6

Retirement and Drug Abuse/Misuse

As we have seen, alcohol abuse and misuse in late life is a serious issue with repercussions at both the individual and social levels. In this chapter, we turn briefly to the related problems of drug abuse/misuse—specifically, illicit drug use and the misuse or abuse of prescription drugs. How widespread is drug abuse/misuse in the older population, and what are the consequences of such behavior for individuals, their families, and society? What individual characteristics and demographic factors might influence the use of illicit drugs or misuse of prescription drugs in late life? And can factors related to retirement be identified as affecting individuals' vulnerability to abusing substances other than alcohol?

Two main categories of substances are at issue here: illicit (or, in other words, illegal) drugs such as marijuana, heroin, and cocaine (Schedule 1 drugs in the United States) and legal but controlled drugs with psychoactive effects—that is, prescription medications. The latter comprise by far the greater portion of psychoactive drugs abused or misused by people in later life. Certain over-the-counter drugs may also be misused, though these are generally not addictive.

First, we will discuss what is known about the extent and epidemiology of substance abuse involving illegal drugs and prescription medications in the older population. In general, this is not a great deal. While the etiology of alcohol problems among older adults has been extensively explored, comparable research on controlled or illegal substances remains limited, with only a handful of studies examining the individual and demographic factors potentially associated with drug abuse. After summarizing this research, we will describe the results of our own analysis (Bacharach, Bamberger, Sonnenstuhl, & Vashdi, 2008b) examining the possible association between retirement and drug abuse in our blue-collar study population.

ILLICIT DRUG USE IN THE OLDER POPULATION

Traditionally, the use of illicit drugs by older adults has been minimal. Data from the 2002 National Survey on Drug Use and Health (NSDUH), based on a sample of 2,019 adults aged 65 and up, show rates of lifetime and previous-year illicit drug use of 9.2% and 1.3%, respectively (Substance Abuse and Mental Health Services Administration, 2003). To put this into context, the comparable figures for alcohol were 78% and 50% (Moore et al., 2009). In general, illicit drug use is highest among people in their teens and early 20s; the subsequent decline tends to already be under way before users reach their 30th birthday (Gfroerer et al., 2003). The initial reduction can be attributed to natural life course shifts that bring new responsibilities, such as work, marriage, and parenthood; over time, the greater morbidity associated with illicit drug use reduces the number of continued users, while the needs and habits of others change as the years pass (Gfroerer et al., 2003). Simoni-Wastila and Yang (2006, p. 381) suggest that "in general, use of illegal drugs by older adults is limited to a small group of aging criminals and long-term heroin addicts." Kennedy et al. (1999, p. 228), citing Barnas, Rossman, Roessler, Reimer, and Fleischhacker (1992), write that "the incidence of addiction to illicit substances after the age of 65 approaches zero, with prevalent cases representing abusers who have aged into geriatric status. Middle-aged opiate addicts more often 'mellow out,' die, transition to alcohol or prescription medications with abuse potential or enter methadone programs."

The aging of the Baby Boom generation seems to be changing this picture somewhat. As is true for alcohol use, people's experiences with illicit drugs during youth help to shape their later attitudes and behavior with regard to these substances (Moore et al., 2009; Reardon, 2012; Wu & Blazer, 2011). That the Baby Boomers engaged in illicit drug use during their teens and 20s at higher rates than previous cohorts is well known, but some figures are instructive. For example, according to the Substance Abuse and Mental Health Services Administration (SAMHSA; 1996, 2000), the rate of illicit drug use in the United States peaked in 1979, when the Baby Boom cohort was aged 15 to 33 (based on a definition of the cohort as those born from 1946 to 1964; other definitions differ slightly). In 1995, when the Boomers were in their 30s and 40s, nearly half that cohort (49%) reported having used illicit drugs during their lifetime, compared with only 11% of all adults aged 50 or above (Gfroerer et al., 2003).

It is unsurprising, then, that the aging of the Baby Boom cohort is accompanied by findings showing increased illicit drug use among Americans in older age groups. For instance, in the peak year of 1979, when the Baby Boomers were all under 34, only 10% of illicit drug users in the country were aged 35 or above. Sixteen years later—that is, in 1995—a full 27% of illicit drug users were 35 or older (Gfroerer et al., 2003). Similarly, Han, Gfroerer, and Colliver (2009) examined national trends of drug use among adults aged 50 to 59 between 2002 and 2007. The percentage of people in their 50s who reported having used marijuana in the past year increased from 3.1% in 2002 to 5.7% in 2007. (The comparable figures for nonmedical prescription drug use showed a similar increase, from 2.2% to 4.4%.)

There is little reason to expect that this pattern will change in the coming years, now that the oldest Boomers are midway through their seventh decade. Moreover, it will be some time before this trend works its way through the system, leaving an older population whose early exposure to illicit drugs more closely resembles that of pre-Boomer cohorts. As Gfroerer et al. (2003) point out, the immediate post-Boomer cohort also engaged in illicit drug use at high rates during their youth. These are the Boomers' younger siblings, cousins, and neighbors, the kids they influenced as scout leaders or camp counselors—now in or nearing middle age.

According to Taylor and Grossberg (2012), while it has "been long assumed that drug habits would diminish and vanish with aging," the profiles of substance abusers have changed considerably over recent decades, and "this pattern no longer appears to hold" (p. 2). However, even with the aging of the Baby Boomers, abuse of Schedule 1 drugs is likely to remain relatively minor compared with at-risk or abusive use of either alcohol or prescription medications. Taylor and Grossberg (2012) also note that the population of elderly substance abusers remains quite small, less than 1%. In addition, their analyses show that nearly all older drug abusers have a long history of substance abuse, with late-onset abuse (i.e., abuse initiated in later life) accounting for less than 10% of substance abuse among the elderly.

Using data from the National Household Surveys on Drug Abuse of 2000 and 2001, Gfroerer et al. (2003) estimated that in those years about 2.3% of American adults aged 50 and above met the diagnostic criteria[1] for dependence on or abuse of either alcohol or illicit drugs. Of these, the vast majority (about 86%) were dependent on or abusing alcohol alone. Ten percent met the criteria for illicit drugs only and 4%, for both illicit drugs and alcohol. Yet the definition of *illicit drugs* used by Gfroerer et al. (2003) is actually broader than is normally suggested by the term. The two most common drugs of abuse identified by that survey were indeed Schedule 1 drugs (marijuana and cocaine, used by 42% and 36%, respectively, of those identified as having drug abuse or dependence problems). But the other groups comprised or could include legal prescription medications: pain relievers (25%), stimulants (18%), and sedatives (17%). Moreover, it is likely that the strict adherence to the *Diagnostic and Statistical Manual of Mental Disorders*, fourth edition (DSM-IV; American Psychiatric Association, 1994) criteria used in the surveys analyzed by Gfroerer et al. (2003) means that they miss a large number of problems related to prescription drug use among older people. It is to such questions that we turn next.

PRESCRIPTION DRUG MISUSE AND ABUSE IN THE OLDER POPULATION

In the United States and throughout the Western world, older people rely heavily on prescription medications. Individuals aged 65 and over account for over one-third of all prescriptions written in the United States, despite making up less than 15% of the population (Basca, 2008; Simoni-Wastila & Yang, 2006). The sheer number of Baby Boomers means that over the coming years more people in their seventh, eighth, and ninth decades will be using psychoactive drugs for medical purposes and, indeed, may be taking several different drugs for different conditions. In the year 2000, almost half of all Americans aged 65 and up were taking three or more prescription drugs, up from one-third in 1988 (Basca, 2008). Some older people fill upward of 20 prescriptions per year, from four or five different therapeutic classes (Simoni-Wastila & Yang, 2006).

To a great extent, today's elderly (at least in more developed countries) have these medications to thank for their longevity. Yet, as is so often the case, there is truth to the adage "there can be too much of a good thing." There are two areas of concern: the risk of adverse reactions arising in the context of drugs taken for therapeutic purposes and the possibility of abuse or dependence. *Adverse reactions* are defined as detrimental side effects that occur when a drug is taken as prescribed or directed or as the result of a drug–drug or drug–alcohol interaction where the drug or drugs were taken in accordance with directions. The physiological changes associated with aging (including decreased liver and kidney function) and the fact that older adults often take multiple medications make this age group more likely than younger people to experience serious adverse reactions to pharmaceuticals. According to the Drug Abuse Warning Network (DAWN) report of February 24, 2011,[2] more than 1,100,000 emergency department visits were made in 2008 by older adults (aged 50 and up) for adverse reactions to medications, 60% of them by people over 64. Nearly 80% of the visits involved only one pharmaceutical, almost 14% involved two, and just under 7% involved three or more pharmaceuticals. About 1% involved a combination of pharmaceuticals and alcohol. Nearly two-thirds of the older adults in these visits were treated and released, nearly one-third were admitted to the hospital, and less than 4% were admitted to the intensive care unit (Substance Abuse and Mental Health Services Administration, 2011).

Yet while the risk of adverse drug–drug and drug–alcohol reactions is serious and costly, it can be approached by improving awareness of potential side effects and monitoring of the drugs taken by older adults on the part of the medical professionals and family members who care for them (Substance Abuse and Mental Health Services Administration, 2011). In this respect, it is to be distinguished from the more insidious problem of drug abuse and dependence.

In contrast to younger people, who may take psychoactive prescription drugs deliberately in order to get high, older people who develop patterns of abuse and dependence tend to do so inadvertently, following a path from appropriate use through misuse to abuse (Simoni-Wastila & Yang, 2006). The pattern can begin in seemingly innocuous ways. For example, older people forget whether they took their usual pill with breakfast, so they take another one. Or perhaps they wake up feeling worse than usual, so they take two pills on purpose, thinking that will help. (Recall the flight attendant mentioned in chapter 5 who took two different sleeping pills each night, one to relax her muscles and the other to help her fall asleep.) They have a headache, so they take the prescribed painkiller left over from their recent knee surgery. Or a friend offers them some sleeping pills, thinking she's doing them a favor. All of these things can lead to abuse and physical dependence.

Table 6.1 lists the prescription medications commonly taken by people in late life with the greatest potential for abuse or dependence.[3] Most important in terms of the probable numbers of people affected are opioids and benzodiazepines. Opioids are analgesics that are obtained from the resin of the opium poppy or produced synthetically in the laboratory; either way, they have the same potential for addiction as the illegal opiate heroin. Opioids effectively reduce the perception of pain and produce a strong feeling of euphoria. They are invaluable in the management of the chronic, disabling pain associated with advanced cancer or with degenerative conditions such as rheumatoid arthritis; but they may also be prescribed for short-term use, as for hip fractures. The most commonly prescribed opioids

Table 6.1. PRESCRIPTION DRUGS THAT ARE SUBJECT TO ABUSE AND
DEPENDENCE IN OLDER ADULTS

Drug	Prescribed for
Benzodiazepines	
Long-acting: flurazepam, diazepam	Anxiety
Short-acting: alprazolam, lorazepam, triazolam, temazepam	Insomnia and other sleep problems
Barbiturate and nonbarbiturate sedative hypnotics	
Pentobarbital, secobarbital, aprobarbital/ secobarbital, chloral hydrate, ethchlorvynol, glutethimide	Anxiety and sleep problems
Opioid analgesics	
Morphine, levorphanol, methadone, codeine, hydrocodone, oxycodone, propoxyphene, fentanyl, tramadol	Pain relief
Central nervous system stimulants	
Methylphenidate, methamphetamine, dextroamphetamine, amphetamine-dextroamphetamine	Narcolepsy and attention-deficit/hyperactivity disorder; used off-label to treat depression

Note. Adapted from Simoni-Wastila, L., & Yang, H. K. (2006). Psychoactive drug abuse in older adults. *American Journal of Geriatric Pharmacotherapy, 4,* 380–394.

are hydrocodone (trade names Vicodin, Lortab, and Lorcet) and oxycodone (trade names OxyContin, Percodan, and Percocet). Benzodiazepines are a type of central nervous system depressant, or sedative. They slow down normal brain functioning and are used to treat sleep problems and anxiety. Benzodiazepines include diazepam (trade names include Valium), chlordiazepoxide (Librium), alprazolam (Xanax), and triazolam (Halcion). These are among the most frequently prescribed psychiatric medications; studies suggest that between 9% and 54% of older adults use benzodiazepines in any given year (Wu & Blazer, 2011). Both opioids and benzodiazepines can lead to tolerance and physical dependence in older adults, even when taken at appropriate doses for appropriate amounts of time, so usage must be managed carefully and discontinued gradually so as not to cause withdrawal symptoms (Simoni-Wastila & Yang, 2006).

How many people are affected by prescription drug disorders (i.e., abuse and dependence)? Nobody really knows. One study conducted by SAMHSA found that in 2001 300,000 adults aged over 55 engaged in nonmedical use of more than one prescription drug over the past month. Another study, from the National Center on Addiction and Substance Abuse, estimated that 2.8 million American women aged 60 and above misuse psychoactive prescription drugs each year (Simoni-Wastila & Yang, 2006). However, these figures deal with use and misuse, not with abuse and dependence, which are less yielding to standard survey methods. Unfortunately, as we saw with regard to alcohol, the symptoms of prescription drug abuse and dependence can resemble physical and cognitive impairments commonly associated with aging: disorientation, memory loss, poor balance, shaky hands, and mood swings or depression (Basca, 2008). This means that many, if not most, cases of prescription drug disorders among older adults—possibly upward of 60%, as suggested by Basca (2008)—likely go unrecognized.

Wu and Blazer (2011) report on studies by themselves and others that expose trends in prescription drug abuse and dependence. In one of their own studies (Blazer & Wu, 2009c), they used the 2005–2006 NSDUH to analyze data on past-year nonmedical use and abuse of various drug classes by adults aged 50 and up. Prescription opioids were used by 1.4% of the sample, compared with figures of less than 0.5% for each of three other classes (sedatives, tranquilizers, and stimulants). Among those who used opioids for nonmedical purposes, about half said they had initiated such use between ages 18 and 39, another 16% did so between ages 40 and 49, and 21% initiated use at age 50 or later. The authors estimated that 1 in 13 of the older adults in the sample (7.6%) were at risk of developing opioid dependence. With regard to benzodiazepines, one survey of nearly 2,800 community-dwelling adults aged 65 and over in Canada found that 3.3% of the women and 0.8% of the men met DSM-IV criteria for past-year benzodiazepine dependence; among the subsample of benzodiazepine users, almost 1 in 10 met the dependence criteria (Préville et al., 2008; Voyer, Préville, Roussel, Berbiche, & Beland, 2009).

Health care providers are partly to blame for this problem. Even if the patient follows prescription instructions to the letter, doctors can contribute to drug dependence by prescribing a drug at a higher dose or for a longer duration than required or prescribing multiple drugs from the same therapeutic class (Simoni-Wastila & Yang, 2006). Older patients may request, and doctors may prescribe, opioids and benzodiazepines to help them cope with normal aspects of aging, such as altered sleep–wake cycles (a product of changes in melatonin levels) or mood changes, that might be amenable to other therapies (Basca, 2008). Lack of coordination between different specialists who treat patients for different conditions compounds the problem. Health care providers need to be alert to the possibility of prescription drug dependence and to the ways patients can manipulate the system so as to gain access to psychoactive drugs: e.g., "doctor shopping" (obtaining multiple prescriptions from different providers and filling them at different pharmacies), using unregulated Internet suppliers, or obtaining leftover medications from family members or friends to whom they were legitimately prescribed.

It is important to stress that even if the number of people affected by prescription drug abuse and dependence is relatively small, the consequences of the problem are not—either for the individuals and their families or in terms of the cost to the health care system from, for example, emergency department visits, hospitalizations, and lab tests. According to Basca (2008), health problems related to substance abuse among people aged 65 and above cost Medicare $233 million in 1989, a figure that is probably significantly higher today. To combat this human and financial toll, we need to determine who is likely to be at risk—and who is likely to benefit from prevention and treatment interventions.

WHO IS AT RISK?

As we noted at the beginning of this chapter, there is a paucity of research on the etiology of psychoactive drug disorders and the factors that might affect an individual's vulnerability to abuse, dependence, or misuse. The literature reveals a few broad patterns. First, surveys suggest that, as with alcohol, the risk is greater among the younger old. For instance, Blazer and Wu (2009b, 2009c) found that adults aged 50 to 64 use more psychoactive drugs than those 65 or older. Looking at specific substances, the comparative rates of past-year use for the 50-to-65 and 65-plus age groups found by Blazer and Wu were 3.9% versus 0.7% for marijuana and 0.7% versus 0.04% for cocaine. The 50-to-64 age group engaged in nonmedical opioid use at a rate of 1.9% compared with 1.4% for all respondents aged 50 and over (Wu & Blazer, 2011). Yet it should be noted that the data used for these analyses date from 2005 and 2006, before the Baby Boomers began to turn 65.

Not many studies have examined gender differences in substance use and dependence among older adults, but the available literature suggests that such differences do exist. Older men are more likely than older women to use illegal drugs (Wu & Blazer, 2011). However, older women appear to be more likely to misuse and to become dependent on prescription drugs (Simoni-Wastila & Yang, 2006; Wu & Blazer, 2011). Earlier, we mentioned Préville et al.'s (2008) finding that 3.3% of the women but only 0.8% of the men in their sample met DSM-IV criteria for past-year benzodiazepine dependence. In general, two relevant points can be gleaned from various studies: (1) older women are more likely than older men to be prescribed psychoactive medications, particularly benzodiazepines, and to use them for long periods of time and (2) in general, younger and middle-aged women have a greater lifetime risk of dependence on antianxiety medications (benzodiazepines and sedative hypnotics) than do men (Simoni-Wastila & Yang, 2006). Generalizing the latter point in light of the former, it appears that being female is a risk factor for developing or maintaining a psychoactive drug use disorder in later life. This may have to do partly with men's apparent preference for alcohol as a means of self-medication, as we have already seen in this volume.

Blazer and Wu (2009b, 2009c) identified a number of other sociodemographic factors associated with greater illegal drug use or misuse/abuse of prescription drugs. Survey respondents who were not married (whether widowed, divorced, or never married) were more likely to use illegal drugs (specifically marijuana and cocaine). Individuals who had suffered an episode of major depression during the past year were more likely to use illegal drugs and to misuse prescription opioids. In addition, people who consumed alcohol or used marijuana were more likely to misuse opioids. Other studies have found similar associations between a diagnosed psychoactive drug disorder and a diagnosed alcohol use disorder and/or anxiety or depression (Simoni-Wastila & Yang, 2006). It should be recalled that these analyses reveal relationships but say nothing about causality, leaving open the question of whether these associations involve a direct causal relationship, mere correlation, or (more likely) a mutual feedback loop.

As of this writing, there is almost no published research examining the possible link between work-related factors (including disengagement from work) and drug abuse among alder adults. We took advantage of the large sample of retirement-eligible blue-collar workers recruited for our project on alcohol use and retirement to address, in one study, how older workers' chosen retirement trajectories might impact their vulnerability to abusing psychoactive drugs. This study is described in the next section.

RETIREMENT TRAJECTORY, AGE, AND DRUG ABUSE

In our study (Bacharach, Bamberger, Sonnenstuhl, & Vashdi, 2008b), we examined whether retirement serves as a risk factor for drug abuse and whether age and retirement trajectory condition this relationship. By *retirement trajectory*, we meant whether an individual (1) retired as soon as he or she became eligible, (2) deferred retirement and continued working in his or her career job, or (3) retired and engaged in bridge employment. By *drug abuse*, we meant either the nonmedical use of either over-the-counter or prescription medications, the deliberate use of such medications in excess of the directions, or the use of illegal drugs.

We expected age to have an attenuating effect on any relationship between retirement and the severity of drug abuse, for several reasons. First, those interested in retiring at the first opportunity (i.e., at the youngest possible age) may include individuals who already misuse or abuse drugs. These individuals are most likely to view retirement as insurance against being fired and thus losing their benefits. Second, those retiring at a younger age may do so at least in part for health reasons. These early retirees may be at increased risk of more severe drug abuse, particularly if they have physical or psychological problems for which they have been taking drugs or if their health has forced them into retirement with insufficient economic security (in which case they may turn to drugs to self-medicate financial strain).

We further expected that the attenuation effect of age would be reinforced to the extent that older workers defer their retirement. That is, we argued that retirement-eligible workers who delay retirement and continue to work may also be at a heightened risk of drug abuse. Such workers may be forced to stay on the job for financial reasons and may turn to drugs to self-medicate financial strain. Alternatively, older workers may use drugs to help them cope with the increasingly challenging physical demands of the job (whether heavy lifting or manipulating small objects) and the physical pain often accompanying such demands. In other words, drug problems may become more likely as retirement-eligible workers defer retirement and age on the job. This, in turn, should weaken any link between retirement and drug abuse.

Finally, we expected age to exert a weaker attenuation effect on the retirement–drug abuse relationship among those opting for bridge employment. That is, we reasoned that the ability of younger retirees to abuse drugs is likely to be limited to the extent that they opt to remain in the workforce after retiring, while at the same time older people opting for bridge employment may face some of the same concerns as those deferring retirement and, hence, be motivated to use drugs in a similar manner (e.g., to self-medicate physical job demands or financial strain).

For this study, we analyzed data from 978 respondents in our main study (661 men and 317 women) collected about 3.5 years after they became eligible for retirement. Five hundred and forty-one respondents (55%) were fully retired, 295 (30%) had chosen to defer retirement, and 142 (15%)

Table 6.2. MODIFIED DRUG ABUSE SCREENING TEST (DAST)

1. Do you use more than one drug at a time in excess of the directions?
2. Are you unable to stop using drugs when you want to?
3. Have you ever had blackouts or flashbacks as a result of drug use?
4. Do you ever feel bad or guilty about your drug use?
5. Is your spouse ever concerned about your use of drugs in excess of the directions or inappropriately?
6. Does the use of drugs cause you to neglect your family?
7. Have you ever experienced withdrawal symptoms (felt sick) when you stopped taking drugs?
8. Have you had medical problems as a result of your drug use (e.g., memory loss, hepatitis, convulsions, bleeding)?

Note. Adapted from Skinner, H. A. (1982). The Drug Abuse Screening Test. *Addictive Behaviors, 7*, 363–371.

were engaged in full- or part-time bridge employment. The participants fell into six age categories, from 39–43 (the youngest) to 64–70 (the oldest); most were in the middle age ranges. We measured drug abuse based on an eight-question version of the Drug Abuse Screening Test (DAST; Skinner, 1982), an instrument designed to assess abuse of substances other than alcohol over the previous 12 months (see Table 6.2).[4] Twenty-six percent of the respondents answered "yes" to at least one question on the DAST, meaning they had a least one problem related to drug abuse. Over 2% answered "yes" to at least six questions, representing a level of addiction high enough to warrant formal clinical assessment.

The results of the analyses draw a picture of retirement as having a generally positive association with drug abuse. Being fully retired, as opposed to fully employed, was associated with increased severity of drug abuse, after controlling for gender, age, marital status, and whether the participant had been hospitalized over the past year (see Table 6.3, model 2). In addition, and surprisingly, individuals opting for bridge retirement reported levels of drug abuse not significantly different from those reported by individuals deferring retirement altogether. That is, in contrast to our expectations, we found that retirement was linked to the severity of drug abuse only to the extent that retirees completely disengaged from the workforce.

As we anticipated, the impact of retirement on drug abuse seems to depend upon the individual's age. This is evident from the significant interaction between retirement and age shown in model 3 of Table 6.3. Moreover, as shown in Figure 6.1 and Table 6.4, greater age was associated with more severe drug abuse among those deferring retirement and with less severe drug abuse among those who had fully retired.

Table 6.3. THE IMPACT OF AGE AND RETIREMENT ON DRUG ABUSE[a]

Effect	Model 1: Control variables (n = 968)		Model 2: W/retirement (n = 968)		Model 3: W/moderation of age (n = 968)	
	Estimate	Standard error	Estimate	Standard error	Estimate	Standard error
Intercept	−1.11	0.51	−1.30	0.51	−2.04	0.70
Age	0.06	0.07	0.03	0.08	0.23	0.15
Married	0.06	0.16	0.06	0.16	0.07	0.16
Hospitalization	0.20	0.17	0.19	0.17	0.20	0.17
Gender	−0.27	0.16	−0.21	0.16	−0.22	0.16
Fully retired vs. still working			0.36*	0.16	7.71*	0.68
Bridge employment vs. still working			0.30	0.21	0.27	0.80
Age × fully retired					−0.34*	0.17
Age × bridge employment					0.02	0.21
Random effect of employment sector	0.18	0.21	0.74	0.16	0.67	0.16
−2Log likelihood	4,064.84		4,048.83		4,026.31	
Δ−2Log likelihood			16.01***		22.52***	

Note. [a]Negative binomial hierarchical linear modeling regression with Drug Abuse Screening Test as the dependent variable. Reprinted from Addictive Behaviors, 33, Bacharach S., Bamberger P., Sonnenstuhl, W., & Vashdi, D., Retirement and drug abuse: The conditional role of age and retirement trajectory, 1610–1614, Copyright 2008, with permission of Elsevier.
*$p < .05$, **$p < .01$, ***$p < .001$.

The mean DAST score for those retiring early on (i.e., before age 49, groups 1 and 2) is more than twice as high as the mean score for those retiring after the age of 54 (groups 4, 5, and 6). Meanwhile, workers in the younger age groups (i.e., 40s through mid-50s; groups 1–4) who deferred retirement reported fewer drug-related problems than their older employed peers (groups 5 and 6).

In short, overall, for those who had fully retired, age was inversely related to drug abuse severity, with younger retirees reporting more abuse-related problems than older retirees. The relationship was reversed for those who deferred retirement and remained employed at their primary workplaces. However, it should be noted that even among the group with the highest DAST scores—i.e., young retirees—the mean DAST score was still quite low, under 1.0.

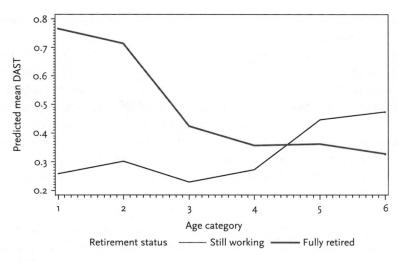

Figure 6.1:
The Moderating Effect of Retirement Status on the Relationship Between Age and Drug Abuse.
Source: Reprinted from Addictive Behaviors, 33, Bacharach S., Bamberger P., Sonnenstuhl, W., & Vashdi, D., Retirement and drug abuse: The conditional role of age and retirement trajectory, 1610–1614, Copyright 2008, with permission of Elsevier.

SUMMARY AND CONCLUSION

As we just described, the findings of our study point to a generally positive association between retirement and drug abuse. Yet a closer look at the data reveals that drug abuse is likely to be more severe among two groups of people: those who retire at a relatively young age and those who age on

Table 6.4. MEAN DRUG ABUSE SCREENING TEST SCORES (AND STANDARD DEVIATIONS) BY AGE GROUP AND WORKING STATUS

	Still working			Fully retired		
Age category	n	Mean	SD	n	Mean	SD
1 b: 1957–1963	6	0.26	0.05	3	0.76	0.09
2 b: 1952–1956	27	0.30	0.08	11	0.71	0.10
3 b: 1947–1951	175	0.23	0.09	84	0.42	0.12
4 b: 1942–1946	160	0.28	0.11	165	0.36	0.10
5 b: 1937–1941	63	0.45	0.13	266	0.36	0.06
6 b: 1930–1936	6	0.47	0.05	7	0.33	0.09

Note. SD = standard deviation. Reprinted from Addictive Behaviors, 33, Bacharach S., Bamberger P., Sonnenstuhl, W., & Vashdi, D., Retirement and drug abuse: The conditional role of age and retirement trajectory, 1610–1614, Copyright 2008, with permission of Elsevier.

the job despite being eligible for retirement. These findings have a number of implications.

First, they reinforce other findings from our study suggesting that there is likely to be, so to speak, an optimal time to retire from the individual's point of view and that workers who retire earlier or later than this optimal time are likely to do so because of sources of stress in their lives—for example, retiring early for health reasons or remaining on the job because of financial concerns. For those who retire early, it is likely not retirement per se that drives the relationship with drug abuse but the conditions that underlie the decision to retire. This might be (among other possibilities) a health condition which simultaneously (1) motivates a pattern of drug use that can lead to abuse or dependence (e.g., to relieve pain) and (2) creates the conditions that enable access to drugs with abuse potential (e.g., prescription pain relievers). Likewise, for those retiring later, it is not necessarily the decision to delay retirement per se that drives drug abuse but the conditions which underlie that decision (e.g., financial strain) or are created by it (e.g., the physical difficulty of blue-collar work with advancing age).

Second, our findings imply that it is not enough to look for a simple relationship between age and drug abuse, as suggested by previous research findings which point to a greater risk of developing drug disorders among the younger old. That is, it may be true that people in their 60s are more likely to develop a drug problem than people in their 70s; but this fact, by itself, does not help us determine which 60-year-olds are most at risk and, therefore, most likely to benefit from prevention and treatment interventions. Our research suggests that an individual's retirement trajectory is one factor that, considered along with age, can help target interventions to where they will be most useful.

In general, our findings give credence to the public health call for a shift in focus among treatment planners to address the special needs of an older population of substance abusers. Moreover, they suggest that the workplace might be an effective arena for intervention and counseling with older adults. Such counseling might help older workers find other means besides self-medication to cope with the physical and psychological strains associated with work or impending retirement. It is to this issue—interventions aimed at preventing substance abuse and misuse among older workers and retirees or treating those who have already developed problems—to which we turn next.

NOTES

1. The criteria for drug abuse or dependence in the *Diagnostic and Statistical Manual of Mental Disorders* (fourth edition) are essentially the same as the criteria for alcohol abuse and dependence shown in Table 1.3, only with "substance use" replacing "alcohol use."

2. DAWN is a public health surveillance system administered by SAMHSA; it monitors drug-related emergency department visits in the United States.

3. Not all psychoactive drugs taken by older people have dependency potential. For instance, antidepressants and antipsychotics are not addictive (Simoni-Wastila & Yang, 2006). Nevertheless, like all substances, they may lead to habituation (Duhigg, 2012).

4. The version of the DAST that we used normally includes 10 items, two of which deal with illicit drug use or illegal activity relating to drug use. Based on concerns voiced by focus group participants about the effect of these items on older respondents, we removed them from the survey.

CHAPTER 7

Helping the Troubled Retiree

In this volume, we have summarized much of what we know about how, when, and under what conditions retirement is likely to play a role in the development or aggravation of alcohol-related problems and other forms of substance abuse. In the current chapter, we will look at interventions aimed at preventing or treating substance misuse and abuse in older adults, and we will ask whether what we have learned about the relationship between retirement and alcohol use might be parlayed into helping improve such interventions. Then, we will consider the implications of these considerations for human resource management in contemporary organizations.

As we've noted, the problem of substance misuse and abuse in older adults is important and growing more so. The number of Americans aged 50 and over who need treatment for substance use disorders is projected to rise from 1.7 million in 2000 to 4.4 million in 2020—the result of a 50% increase in the number of older adults and a 70% increase in their rate of treatment need (Gfroerer et al., 2003). Yet even now, only a small percentage of those needing treatment for substance use disorders actually receive it: Gfroerer et al. (2003) suggest that only 11.9% of the 1.7 million older adults with substance abuse treatment needs at the start of the millennium received such treatment within the past year. This is not a situation that augurs well for controlling health care costs and preserving the nation's economic and social stability.

It should be clear from the outset that when dealing with alcohol misuse and alcohol use disorders, prevention and treatment are equally valid and important goals. (For simplicity's sake, we will speak only of alcohol use in the rest of this chapter, though most of what follows is potentially applicable to drug abuse and misuse as well.) That is, someone who is already dependent on alcohol need not be written off as a lost cause. This is because many of the adverse consequences of heavy drinking are reversible once consumption is halted or reduced. Oslin (2000) describes two studies set in Department of Veterans Affairs nursing homes in which outcomes for veterans who had recently abused alcohol were significantly better than outcomes for veterans with no history of alcohol abuse or dependence (the outcomes were discharge from a nursing home care unit and improvements in day-to-day functioning; Joseph, Atkinson, & Ganzini, 1995, and Oslin, Streim, Parmelee, Boyce, & Katz, 1997, respectively). The findings suggest that "alcohol caused an excess of disability that rapidly reversed in a setting of abstinence" (Oslin, 2000, p. 136). Adams (2002), in her review of the potential medical complications of heavy drinking, also points out that "alcohol-induced illness is often reversible, especially if it is discovered early" (p. 33). She highlights alcohol-related hypertension and dementia as two of the more serious alcohol-related conditions that improve when alcohol intake is decreased; indeed, she notes, alcohol dependence is "probably one of the few truly reversible causes of dementia" (p. 35). Such improvements are likely to translate not only into a better quality of life for the individual but also into savings for society at large, by reducing the cost of long-term elder care.

There is a growing body of literature on the treatment and prevention of alcohol misuse and dependence among older adults (e.g., Barrick & Connors, 2002; Barry et al., 2001; Gurnack, Atkinson, & Osgood, 2002; Kennedy et al., 1999). We will not attempt to summarize this literature in its entirety but will present a brief overview of the most important psychosocial and pharmaceutical interventions in use today. We will then ask whether treatment and prevention programs can profitably be constructed specifically around the adjustment to retirement.

PSYCHOSOCIAL INTERVENTIONS

Three main types of psychosocial interventions for alcohol misuse and disorders are discussed in the literature: screening and brief interventions in the primary care setting, cognitive behavioral therapy, and group therapy programs such as Alcoholics Anonymous (AA). We will discuss each of these briefly in turn, highlighting what we know about their applicability to older adults with a problem of substance misuse or abuse.

Brief interventions are "time-limited, patient-centered counseling strategies" that focus on helping patients change their behavior to meet a particular therapeutic goal (Fleming, 2002, p. 93). Born out of the pressures of the managed care environment, with its expectations of high-quality care delivered within a heavily constrained time frame (Barry et al., 2001), brief interventions are used routinely to help patients lose weight, stop smoking, control their cholesterol or blood pressure, and adhere to medication protocols, as well as to cut down on their drinking (Fleming, 2002). While there is no single model of a brief intervention, the method typically involves up to four sessions lasting 5 to 15 minutes each over a period of 6 to 8 weeks. Often, a scripted manual or workbook is used, to ensure consistency in the intervention regardless of the particular clinician's skills or training. Recent studies point to the efficacy of Internet-based screening and brief interventions—involving little or no clinician involvement—as well (Cunningham, Wild, Cordingley, van Mierlo, & Humphreys, 2009; Neighbors, Lee, Lewis, Fossos, & Walter, 2009; Newton, Teesson, Vogl, & Andrews, 2010). To date, however, we are unaware of any study examining the efficacy of Internet-based screening and brief interventions among older adults.

Within the context of alcohol use, brief interventions reflect two important and related developments in the United States over recent decades. First, in the past, abstinence was often regarded as the sole legitimate goal for people with any type of alcohol-related problem. Today, while abstinence is still considered the appropriate goal in cases of alcohol dependence, as a rule the focus on abstinence has been replaced by a "harm reduction public health paradigm," aimed at reducing alcohol use to low-risk levels (Fleming, 2002, p. 90). Under the public health paradigm, practitioners recognize that most people with actual or potential alcohol-related problems do not meet the criteria for alcohol dependence, and a low-risk approach can help keep their drinking within safe limits.

This development has worked in tandem with the shift to a managed care approach to change the role of primary care providers vis-à-vis alcohol misuse. Formerly, it was the role of the physician to identify patients with alcohol use disorders and refer them for specialized (often inpatient) treatment. Today, the primary care practice is increasingly the setting in which at-risk or problem drinkers are helped to recognize the risks or problems associated with their drinking and to change their drinking behavior (Fleming, 2002).

The process begins with screening. Patients coming in for routine visits are asked questions about the quantity and frequency of their drinking,

Table 7.1. THE CAGE SCREENING TOOL

C = Have you ever felt you ought to Cut down on your drinking?

A = Have people Annoyed you by criticizing your drinking?

G = Have you felt bad or Guilty about your drinking?

E = Do you need an Eye-opener first thing in the morning?

possibly accompanied by one of the various available screening tests for problem drinking—for example, the CAGE (Table 7.1) or the Drinking Problems Index (DPI, Table 1.4).[1] Screening can take place in person, by telephone, or via an online or pencil-and-paper questionnaire in the waiting room (Barry et al., 2001; Fleming, 2002).[2] Patients who screen positive for at-risk or problem drinking can then be given a more complete evaluation to determine whether they are likely to benefit from an in-house brief intervention or whether referral to a more intensive inpatient or outpatient program is appropriate.

It should be noted that in screening an older population, the CAGE and the DPI both offer an advantage over other tools, such as the MAST and AUDIT, in that the latter include items which may be less relevant for some older adults (e.g., questions on the work-related consequences of drinking). However, Finney et al. (1991) concluded that the CAGE, too, may offer limited sensitivity for an older population, in that it fails to "tap adverse consequences from drinking that are more likely to occur among older adults" (p. 396). (*Sensitivity* is the degree to which an instrument correctly identifies those individuals who have a given condition or, in other words, the degree to which the proportion of false negatives is minimized. It is to be distinguished from *specificity*—the degree to which the instrument correctly identifies those individuals who do not have the condition or, in other words, the degree to which the proportion of false positives is minimized.) Finney et al. (1991) developed the DPI specifically to assess drinking problems in older adults and showed it to have high levels of internal reliability and construct validity. In our own study (Bamberger et al., 2006), we found that the DPI does indeed seem to provide enhanced accuracy relative to the CAGE in distinguishing between older adults with and without drinking problems. Notably, in our study, sensitivity was considerably higher for the DPI than for the CAGE across four of five outcome parameters (the exception being liver disease) with a cutoff score of 1 or 2. In addition, the CAGE failed to simultaneously present good sensitivity and specificity with respect to the four outcomes, while the DPI was able to do so, particularly when its cutoff was set at 1.

As described, screening and, where needed, further evaluation can identify those patients deemed likely to benefit from a brief intervention. These are characterized by three main features. First, the method encourages compliance by involving the patient as an active partner. For instance, the process typically begins with some form of goal setting or contracting, where the clinician and the patient together negotiate an achievable target for behavior change. A second, related feature is the method's nonconfrontational approach, where the clinician relies on motivational interviewing or similar collaborative, noncoercive techniques rather than "doctor's orders" to persuade patients of the need for change. Motivational interviewing involves a semistructured set of questions and responses designed to help patients recognize the risks associated with their current behavior, internalize the need for change, and develop a commitment to that change. Motivational interviewing is "a supportive, respectful approach that is persuasive without being coercive or cajoling and is particularly relevant in working with older patients" (Barry et al., 2001, p. 14).

Finally, interventions often place an emphasis on social norming (Osilla, Zellmer, Larimer, Neighbors, & Marlatt, 2008). Based on the assumption that some older adults may drink primarily for social reasons, with excessive drinking maintained mainly by misconceptions of peer drinking norms, brief interventions are often structured to address such misconceptions. As we have noted in earlier chapters, alcohol misuse among the retirees that we studied is often influenced by the retirees' perception of how much and how often their peers consume (descriptive norms) as well as by perceptions of how much others approve of their substance use (injunctive norms). Research suggests that misperceptions about such norms can be addressed by providing older adults with feedback about how much their peers or others in their age cohort drink and then helping them compare their own consumption pattern with that of their peers (Barry et al., 2001; Perkins, 1997; Perkins & Berkowitz, 1986).

Barry et al. (2001) propose a semistructured brief intervention specifically designed for older at-risk and problem drinkers. The intervention includes nine steps. In the first step, the older person is asked to identify key goals for the future, in terms of, for example, his or her health, activities, relationships, or financial stability. The identification of goals establishes a context for thinking about the ramifications of drinking and establishes rapport between the patient and the clinician. In the second step, the clinician and patient develop a general picture of the older person's health habits (smoking, nutrition, and so on). This step provides an opportunity for the clinician to deal with other concerns the patient might have and helps to set alcohol use in the context of other health-related behaviors. Steps 3 through 6 allow the clinician to present contextual information on at-risk or problem drinking and how it can affect an older person's physical, psychological, and social functioning (e.g., drinking norms for the patient's age group and the potential benefits of cutting down on drinking). In step 7, the patient and clinician together determine drinking limits that the patient is comfortable with and feels he or she will be able to achieve. The patient signs a contract to meet these drinking limits and agrees to keep a drinking diary, charting his or her progress. In the eighth step, the clinician and patient identify situations and moods that tend to trigger the patient's drinking (e.g., social isolation, boredom, and negative family interactions) and develop strategies that the patient can use to deal with these as they arise. The session concludes with a summary, a review of the patient's drinking goals, and scheduling a follow-up session in 6 weeks' time. Follow-up sessions are similarly structured and can continue until the patient's drinking is under control or until the patient and clinician decide that more intensive inpatient or outpatient treatment is needed (Barry et al., 2001).

Studies employing randomized controlled designs have found that brief interventions can be effective at reducing alcohol problems in both younger and older adults. One prominent example dealing with younger adults is the Trial for Early Alcohol Treatment, or Project TrEAT (Fleming, Barry, Manwell, Johnson, & London, 1997). Of 17,695 patients visiting 17 primary care practices in Wisconsin, 774 individuals aged between 18 and 64 who screened positive for at-risk or problem drinking were divided into intervention and control groups; 723 took part in the 12-month follow-up. (The criteria excluded people who consumed more than 50 drinks per week, who showed signs of alcohol dependence, or who had been in an alcohol treatment program over the past year.) The intervention comprised two 10- or 15-minute sessions delivered by a primary care physician using a scripted workbook and contracting materials (a drinking agreement and drinking diary cards). The two sessions were 4 weeks apart, and each session was followed 2 weeks later by a 5-minute follow-up phone call from a clinic nurse. Over 1 year, both the control and intervention groups reduced their weekly alcohol consumption (quantity and frequency) and their frequency of binge drinking, but the reductions were significantly greater in the intervention group. In addition, follow-up analyses using various outcome measures found significant differences between the two groups. At 12 months, the intervention group reported fewer emergency department visits (107 vs. 132 by the control group) and fewer days of hospitalization

(126 vs. 326). At 48 months, data from the Wisconsin Department of Transportation showed that participants in the intervention group had been involved in significantly fewer motor vehicle accidents involving fatalities (0 vs. 2), injuries (20 vs. 31), and property damage only (67 vs. 72). A cost–benefit analysis found that the resulting savings in medical and societal costs significantly outweighed the cost of the intervention (in staff training, screening, patients' time and travel costs, etc.; Mundt, 2006).

Project GOAL (Guiding Older Adult Lifestyles) was a modified version of the TrEAT project designed for adults aged 65 and up (Fleming, Manwell, Barry, Adams, & Stauffacher, 1999). Of 6,073 older primary care patients in Wisconsin, 158 who screened positive for alcohol problems or excessive drinking (more than 11 drinks per week for men or 8 for women) were enrolled in the study, of whom 146 participated in the 12-month follow-up; the same exclusion criteria were applied as in Project TrEAT. Half the sample was assigned to an intervention protocol similar to that used in Project TrEAT. Over 1 year, weekly alcohol consumption in the intervention group dropped by about five drinks per week compared with less than one drink per week in the control group. Moreover, the intervention group saw significant falls in binge drinking (measured in terms of both the frequency of binge-drinking episodes and the quantity of alcohol consumed), while in the control group those measures actually rose.

Most recently, Project BRITE (Brief Intervention and Treatment for Elders) tested the efficacy of the screening and brief intervention model on a sample of nearly 3,500 older adults in Florida (Schonfeld et al., 2010). Screening was conducted at senior centers, health fairs, retirement communities, and senior housing sites. Those screening positive were invited to participate in a scripted, counselor-based brief intervention protocol and then rescreened upon discharge and once again at 30 days postdischarge. Prescription medication misuse was the most prevalent substance use problem among those screening positive (877 positive screens), followed by alcohol (556 positive screens), over-the-counter medications (242 positive screens), and illicit substances (46 positive screens). Those who received the brief intervention demonstrated a significant improvement in alcohol and medication misuse, with misuse falling significantly from screening to discharge and then remaining stable at this diminished rate over the 30-day postdischarge assessment period. However, the findings suggest that the brief intervention was more efficacious at treating alcohol misuse and the misuse of over-the-counter medications than the misuse of prescription medications. Among those who screened positive for alcohol problems on the baseline Short Michigan Alcoholism Screening Instrument–Geriatric Version (SMAST-G) screen, only 18.9% were still positive at discharge and follow-up. Similarly, of the 24 participants flagged for over-the-counter misuse at initial screening, 23 (96%) had improved (i.e., were no longer flagged for over-the-counter misuse) by discharge. In contrast, of the 187 participants flagged for prescription medication misuse at baseline, only 60 (32.1%) had improved (no flag) by discharge; the remaining 127 did not improve.

One important feature of successful interventions is that they prepare the patient for the very real possibility of relapse. Relapse rates reported in the literature vary according to the definition used, but 1-year relapse rates in the general adult population range from around 50% to as high as 90%, where the former is based on a return to pretreatment drinking levels and the latter on consumption of a single drink (Barrick & Connors, 2002). Relapse certainly sets the patient back to an earlier stage of the intervention process, but if the patient is prepared for this possibility, it need not be more than a temporary setback. Moreover, while we are unaware of any research on the matter, it stands to reason that periodic brief intervention "boosters"—one- or two-session follow-up interventions aimed at reinforcing the effects of the initial treatment—may be helpful in reducing the risk of relapse.

Cognitive Behavioral Therapy

As suggested by the results presented so far, for some individuals, a brief intervention may not be enough and a more intensive outpatient or inpatient treatment program may be needed (Schonfeld & Dupree, 2002). One approach that has proved effective at reducing relapse rates for both younger and older adults is cognitive behavioral therapy, or CBT (Barrick & Connors, 2002). This type of therapy is aimed at helping patients strengthen their coping skills so that they can deal with sources of stress in their lives without resorting to alcohol (or other drugs). More specifically, a CBT counselor helps patients recognize triggers for drinking, whether these are intrapersonal (e.g., depression, boredom, or loneliness) or interpersonal (e.g., family conflicts). The counselor then helps the patient replace his or her maladaptive coping behavior (i.e., drinking) with more appropriate cognitive and behavioral responses. Like the brief interventions just described, CBT employs a supportive, nonconfrontational approach and semistructured feedback to help the patient change habits of mind that lead to undesired behavior. However, a CBT treatment program typically requires a significant time commitment on the part of the patient—up to several sessions a week for 3 months or more in the active phase of treatment, followed by periodic maintenance sessions. A complete description of CBT is beyond the scope of this volume, but interested readers can find a comprehensive discussion of the technique and its use with older adults in Schonfeld and Dupree (2002).

Group Therapy and Alcoholics Anonymous

Another option for older people with drinking problems or alcohol use disorders is some sort of supportive group therapy, including self-help groups such as AA. For older as well as younger adults, these groups offer opportunities to socialize and engage with other people in an atmosphere that promotes morale and encourages sobriety (Atkinson & Misra, 2002). Indeed, for older people, the social and peer support components of these groups may be more important than any group's particular system or mode of operation, including AA's 12-step program. That is, participation in such groups helps counteract the feelings of depression, loneliness, and boredom that older drinkers often cite as precipitating their drinking (Barrick & Connors, 2002; Schonfeld & Dupree, 2002).

One factor limiting the potential usefulness of support groups like AA for older adults is the relative paucity of such groups that are tailored to an older population. There is evidence that for some older adults, at least, peer-based support groups work best when they really are peer-based—that is, when their members belong to the same age cohort and therefore share similar memories, experiences, and cultural norms (Barrick & Connors, 2002; Kennedy et al., 1999). Atkinson and Misra (2002) point out that mixed-age AA groups also may not suit older people whose mobility is limited (e.g., those who do not drive or go out at night) as such groups are less likely to meet during the working day. However, the number of AA groups with a specifically older-adult membership has been growing since the establishment of the AA's Seniors in Sobriety movement in 1990. According to the 2004 AA membership survey, 16% of AA members were at least 61 years old and 23% were aged 51 through 60, suggesting that the organization's outreach to older adults is likely to grow in the coming years (Alcoholics Anonymous: Seniors in Sobriety, n.d.).

Systematic studies on the effectiveness of AA for older adults are lacking (Atkinson & Misra, 2002). However, Moos, Schutte, et al. (2010) addressed this question as part of their 20-year study into interactions between life stressors, social resources, coping, mental health, and drinking behavior, which we discussed at length in chapter 5. Of the 719 participants who took part in their 20-year survey, about 29% reported at baseline that they had been advised to cut down on their drinking and 43% reported that they had actually tried to cut down. At both the 10- and 20-year follow-ups, at-risk and problem drinking were more likely among respondents who had been advised to cut down on their alcohol intake but were less likely among those who had actually attempted to do so. Further, the authors asked respondents who had tried to reduce their drinking how much support they had received in this endeavor from three sources: family and friends, health professionals (e.g., doctors, psychologists, hospitals, or health clinics), and AA. Only AA proved to be an effective source of help, with support from family, friends, and health professionals proving unrelated to long-term drinking outcomes.

What these findings suggest is that joining a peer-based support program like AA can indeed help older adults reduce or control their drinking if they are motivated to do so. Equally important, the findings show that the motivation to succeed has to be internal. No amount of advice and encouragement will lead someone to curtail their drinking if they are not ready to do so, a fact that is acknowledged in the emphasis on a collaborative, noncoercive approach in brief interventions and CBT. Moos, Schutte, et al.'s (2010) findings also suggest that for people who drink in a social context the positive, social associations of drinking may be stronger than any incentive to curtail alcohol use, even when friends try to support an effort to drink less. This may help explain the effectiveness of AA and similar self-help groups, which integrate the individual into a new support network based on sobriety (Moos, Schutte, et al., 2010).

Interestingly, the role of friends and family is one of the few areas in which Moos and his colleagues identified differences between their final sample (719 respondents) and a comparison group of 582 respondents from the initial sample who completed the 10-year survey but died or dropped out (due to illness or for other reasons) before the 20-year follow-up. For that group, having received help from family and friends in cutting down on alcohol use did presage a lower likelihood of 10-year risky and problem drinking. Because heavy drinking is a risk factor for greater morbidity and mortality, it may be that some of those individuals were in notably poorer health prior to the study and that this circumstance spurred them to take the advice of family and friends to cut down—though, unfortunately, too late.

PHARMACEUTICAL THERAPIES

Some drinkers who fail to respond to psychosocial interventions alone can be helped by pharmaceutical adjuncts—medications that can be used in conjunction with psychosocial therapies to help prevent relapse. The use of such medications is far beyond the scope of this chapter, so we will devote only a few words to them.

There are three main categories of pharmaceutical adjuncts. The first are aversive agents that alter the body's response to alcohol so that consumption of even small amounts of alcohol leads to unpleasant symptoms such as nausea and vomiting. Disulfiram, the most widely prescribed of these deterrent medications, works by inhibiting production of aldehyde dehydrogenase, an enzyme involved in the metabolism of alcohol. The result is a buildup of acetaldehyde, a chemical irritant, in the blood. Placebo-controlled studies of disulfiram have produced mixed results, and the evidence suggests that the drug is fully effective only when taken under conditions of strict compliance. In addition, disulfiram is not suitable for older adults with cardiovascular disease (Barrick & Connors, 2002; Fleming, 2002).

The second category comprises drugs known as opioid receptor antagonists, such as naltrexone. These medications are designed to reduce the reinforcing effects of alcohol by blocking the activity of opioid peptides— amino acids that form part of the brain's reward system and that produce effects similar to opioids such as heroin and morphine. Studies have found that patients taking naltrexone experience less positive effects when they drink (i.e., they get less of an "alcohol high") and have reduced cravings for alcohol (Barrick & Connors, 2002). However, these medications are not suitable for patients being treated for painful health conditions with opioid analgesics (Barrick & Connors, 2002; Fleming, 2002).

Finally, acamprosate is thought to reduce cravings for alcohol in people with alcohol use disorders, though the mechanisms by which it does so are unclear. The drug is believed to stabilize the chemical balance in two neurotransmitter systems that are disrupted by long-term alcohol use (the N-methyl-D-aspartate and gamma-aminobutyric acid systems). Like opioid receptor antagonists, acamprosate seems to reduce the "high" that follows drinking as well as the cravings that accompany withdrawal (Barrick & Connors, 2002). Only a small number of older adults have taken part in studies on acamprosate, so its efficacy and side effects for this population are poorly understood (Fleming, 2002).

PREVENTION AND INTERVENTION USING THE WORK-BASED ASSISTANCE MODEL

All the interventions discussed thus far in this chapter are either community-based or accessed through the health care system and relevant to all older adults regardless of their particular circumstances or stage of life. However, such interventions offer potential solutions only to those who actively seek assistance for their substance-related problem. In the working population, concerns about job retention often serve as a basis for motivating troubled employees to seek help; but once older adults retire, these concerns lose their relevance, and employers or other organizational figures are no longer there to encourage help-seeking. Among the retired, services are typically utilized only by those who self-refer or whose physician, family, or friends convince them to do so, the result being that older adults with an alcohol or other substance use disorder avail themselves of treatment services at rates significantly lower than their younger peers (Bartels, Blow, Brockmann, & Van Citters, 2005). Accordingly, a major concern for policy makers is how retirees may be more effectively motivated to take advantage of the treatment services available to them. We believe that two work-based programs may offer useful starting points for discussion: employee assistance programs (EAPs) and their peer-based counterparts, which we refer to as peer assistance programs (PAPs).

Both EAPs and PAPs are designed to help employees suffering from problems related to alcohol and other substance use, and sometimes other personal problems as well (e.g., marital and parental conflicts, occupational stress, and mental health problems). The basic logic underlying EAPs and PAPs is that the organizational setting is ideal for identifying individuals in need of help because personal problems often manifest themselves through deteriorating performance, such as persistent absenteeism (Golan & Bamberger, 2009). The origins of such programs in the United States date to the early industrial age, when labor unions, relying on principles of volunteerism and mutual aid, took responsibility for helping members in need (Bacharach, Bamberger, & Sonnenstuhl, 2001). Typically, in the early days, assistance was peer-based, unstructured, and informal, with coworkers coming together to offer financial or emotional support to colleagues as the need or occasion arose.

Management-based employee assistance programs became widespread in the United States in the second half of the twentieth century. These programs transferred responsibility for helping troubled employees from informal, peer-based frameworks to formal, management-provided services. While the roots of EAPs are debated, we made the argument over a decade ago (Bacharach et al., 2001) that unions saw advantages in having such programs incorporated in management-provided employee benefits packages and negotiated for this as part of collective bargaining agreements. Further, a National Institute on Alcohol Abuse and Alcoholism campaign in the 1970s encouraged companies to adopt EAPs as a means of combating alcoholism, though these programs also helped employees with other personal issues (Hartwell et al., 1996; Hopkins, 1997; Spell & Blum, 2005). For their part, employers saw these programs as a means to improve workers' performance, enhance productivity, and reduce turnover. To this end, they staffed the programs with professional or credentialed practitioners offering on-site assistance.

In the late 1980s EAPs began to lose favor among employers and workers in the wake of two key trends: the rising cost of health-related benefits, which prompted many firms to contract their EAPs out to external agencies and to transfer control of employees' health benefits to managed care firms, and the widespread adoption of mandatory drug testing by management, which unions regarded as detrimental to the atmosphere of trust and confidentiality needed for employee assistance services to work. The result, at least in unionized enterprises, was a shift to union-based PAPs (also known as "member assistance programs"). Additionally, the peer assistance model has been adopted in enterprises whose employees are not represented by a union (Golan & Bamberger, 2009).

The typical PAP is a voluntary program designed to motivate employees who suffer from substance abuse and other personal problems to seek help and to provide them with support and assistance. Troubled employees can discuss their problems with peer counselors who have been carefully selected for their ability to empathize and ensure confidentiality; many are themselves recovering alcoholics or addicts. These peer counselors are typically trained and coordinated by others serving in a professional capacity—often, union members who have received more extensive training and who are compensated by their union or paid for their time by management. Peer counselors employ both passive and active support roles, in the former case waiting until help is solicited and in the latter seeking out individuals whose behavior has aroused concern. In some cases, clients are referred to the program by a work supervisor following a deterioration in the employee's work performance. Typically, peer counselors are not trained to provide clinical counseling themselves but, rather, serve as empathetic listeners, provide information, and refer clients as needed to professional help services (psychologists, social workers, substance abuse treatment clinics, or self-help organizations).

The types of services offered by EAPs and PAPs can vary in focus, structure, and scope; there is no single model. Some programs focus specifically on substance abuse, while others offer help with a wide variety of personal problems, from elder care to workplace trauma. Some are reactive—that is, aimed at helping employees with existing problems—while others see their mission as prevention and education. Peer counselors may have the authority to refer troubled coworkers directly to outside agencies or clinicians, or they may serve as initial gatekeepers only, referring clients to EAP staff for further assessment and referral. Sometimes, counselors will provide tangible support—such as driving a troubled employee to and from a treatment facility—as well as being there to lend an ear. Programs differ in other ways as well, such as their size and the emphasis they place on follow-up.

From the point of view of the troubled individual, PAPs have various disadvantages and advantages compared with management-based EAPs. On the minus side, the peer counselors, who typically offer their time and energy on a voluntary basis, may be dedicated and empathetic; but they are not professional therapists, and in some cases the most troubled clients may have to undergo a two-stage referral process to get professional help. In contrast, EAPs—at least during their heyday in the 1970s and 1980s—were staffed by credentialed professionals. On the plus side, workers tend to trust peer volunteers and practitioners because they have no interest in using workers' information for discipline-related purposes. In addition, peer counselors may be better positioned than those in management-based programs to motivate workers to seek help because they share the workers' occupational identity and experiences.

We see three potential routes by which the peer assistance model can be modified to better serve the needs of older adults entering retirement. First, these programs can improve their outreach to employees who are nearing the age of retirement eligibility by developing education and interventions aimed at employees who are currently heavy drinkers or who might be at risk for developing drinking problems during the retirement transition. We discuss this further in the section on retirement planning under "Implications for Human Resources Management."

Second, workplace assistance programs might develop specialized services for retirees, specific to this community. To accomplish this, regular program staff (whether paid or volunteers) might be recruited and trained in the special needs of retirees and older adults. Alternatively, peer counselors might be recruited to the PAP from the retiree community itself. This latter strategy may offer a number of significant advantages, in that retiree peer counselors are likely to have a better understanding of the concerns and challenges faced by those they seek to help. They are also likely to be more tightly networked with other retirees (thus giving them greater knowledge of who in the retirement community may be in need of help) and more able to provide follow-up care and companionship to those undergoing or having completed treatment.

Finally, enterprise- or occupation-based retiree organizations may adopt the peer assistance model in order to provide counseling and referral services to their members. For example, existing retiree organizations might establish counseling arms following the peer assistance framework. The Bluebills, the organization of Boeing retirees in the Puget Sound area of Washington, offers a case in point. This organization gives its members access to a retirement assistance program "dedicated to helping fellow Boeing retirees who may have a physical or emotional need" (http://www.bluebills.org/rap.html).

Further inspiration for such organizations might come from the many existing AA groups serving particular occupational sectors, such as International Doctors in AA, International Lawyers in AA, Veterinarians in Recovery, and Birds of a Feather International (an AA group for pilots and cockpit crewmembers).[3] Although retirees are almost always welcome in such occupation-specific AA groups, we are unaware of any such group specifically dedicated to serving the needs of a given occupation's retirees in a given area. Regardless, we view the provision of referral or treatment services to troubled retirees as an important area of activity for any retiree association or occupation-specific AA group.

IMPLICATIONS FOR HUMAN RESOURCES MANAGEMENT

What can organizations do to identify and help older workers or retirees who are at risk of substance misuse? Organizational human resources departments, especially in large, established firms, may be well placed to make a difference for this vulnerable population, by including some of the ideas we have discussed in this chapter in their organizational remit. Given the growing number of older workers in postretirement jobs, one logical step is developing behavioral health programs (or modifying existing ones) so as to target older part-time or contract employees—that is, bridge workers. Another is to integrate substance abuse awareness into retirement planning efforts for older employees. Finally, organizations can reach retired and semiretired workers by expanding the peer assistance model into corporate alumni networks.

Bridge Employees

Bridge employees are, at present, generally underserved by existing employee assistance or behavioral health programs. Only a small number of organizations, to our knowledge, have developed or adopted intervention platforms for older workers, among them bridge employees. In addition, conventional systems of referral to EAPs or PAPs may be ineffective with bridge employees, for several reasons. Supervisors may be less willing to intervene in the case of older workers, out of concerns of being accused of age discrimination. Younger peers and supervisors may feel uncomfortable confronting their seniors. And with bridge employees typically perceived as being temporary, peers and supervisors may fail to be aware of the problem or prefer to simply wait for the problem to go away.

There are several ways in which organizations can identify and assist bridge employees with substance use vulnerabilities. First, they can highlight the health and wellness risks of bridge employment, including substance misuse, as part of the onboarding (organizational socialization) process for older hires, while providing information about how employees can seek help for themselves or their loved ones. Second, they can screen bridge employees for risky substance use behaviors as part of a broader health screening during the hiring or onboarding process. Those identified as engaging in risky behaviors might be referred to an EAP consultant or asked to participate in a brief intervention. Finally, they can develop PAPs that include volunteers from among the workplace community of older employees. These peer counselors should receive training in how to help older, troubled coworkers get the support they need.

Retirement Planning

Organizations can integrate substance abuse awareness into retirement planning for older employees through a two-pronged approach: education and screening. The educational component might involve highlighting the risk factors for substance misuse in retirement as we have discussed them in this book. This can be done in a retirement handbook, at retirement seminars, or in retirement counseling or using any combination of the three.

In addition, organizations can conduct substance misuse screening as part of a broad, preretirement health screening, to identify those who may be at risk. This screening can take place online, either at work or on the employee's own time. Older employees identified as being at risk can then be referred to the appropriate provider or service.

Such efforts have been in place for over a decade in the automobile industry. In one particular enterprise that we studied as part of our broader research into EAPs and PAPs, the director of the plant's PAP designed a 2-hour training session for soon-to-retire employees aimed at preparing them for the challenges they might face in retirement and informing them about the community resources available to them. This training session was executed two or three times a year, depending on the size of the impending retirement cohort. The labor–management PAP for employees of the State of New York offers a similar workshop for those retiring from dozens of state agencies, as well as referral services for retirees in need (http://worklife.ny.gov/).

Alumni Networks

The key to identifying and assessing a substance use problem among retires is having access to them. Once these individuals disengage from work, the employer typically has little contact with them. However, many retirees are more than happy to maintain their work-based social and professional contacts, and this creates an opening for providing help to those who need it.

Corporate alumni networks are groups, either grassroots or company-sponsored, "that help the former employees of a particular organization to maintain their corporate connections" (Koc-Menard, 2009, p. 9). Often, these networks target talented employees who have moved on to other opportunities or who have had to be let go for financial reasons (not a rare occurrence during economic downturns, especially for smaller firms). But alumni networks are increasingly targeting retirees as well. From the organization's perspective, retired organizational alumni offer a rich source of organizational knowledge that can be called upon by less experienced current employees. In addition, these networks can be used to recruit and "re-recruit" talent from among potential bridge employees—that is, retirees interested in continuing to work on a contract basis or in some other capacity (Canabou, 2002; Koc-Menard, 2009).

Enterprises interested in facilitating the development of an alumni network typically need only get a handful of well-connected alumni on board and then support their efforts to reconnect with other alumni (e.g., by sponsoring a reunion). Social media, such as Facebook and LinkedIn, can also be exploited to quickly build and expand such a network.

Once established, alumni networks offer retirees a means to keep in touch with former colleagues, a platform on which to build retiree interest groups or clubs, and a source of job-related information. More important for our purposes in this volume, alumni networks can also be used to initiate or promote a PAP for retirees with a substance misuse problem. Our suggestions for how the work-based peer assistance model might be adapted for enterprise- or occupation-based retiree organizations—following examples such as the Retirement Assistance Program of the Bluebills, the organization of Boeing retirees—are highly relevant here.

SUMMARY AND CONCLUSION

As this book has described, retirement is a potential trigger of new or increased drinking problems or alcohol use disorders among older adults. With the aging of the population, the number of retirees facing such problems is only going to grow. Improving our understanding of the most effective options for treatment, early intervention, and, where possible, prevention of substance misuse and disorders in this population is a vital task facing researchers and practitioners alike.

In this respect, the main problem is not coming up with new programs and protocols. There are good, effective treatment and intervention models out there. The problem is getting older adults to take advantage of treatment and intervention services and providing the necessary follow-up to ensure that they stick with the program or protocol (in the literature, these are known as *utilization* and *continuance*, respectively).

Bartels et al. (2005, pp. 12–13) cite six features that should be incorporated into substance abuse treatment for older adults, drawn from a treatment improvement protocol of the Center for Substance Abuse Treatment, a department of Substance Abuse and Mental Health Services Administration (Center for Substance Abuse Treatment, 1998):

- Age-specific group treatment that is supportive and nonconfrontational
- A focus on coping with depression, loneliness, and loss
- A focus on rebuilding the client's social support network
- A pace and content of treatment appropriate for the older person
- Staff members who are interested and experienced in working with older adults
- Linkages with medical services, services for the aging, and institutional settings for referral into and out of treatment, as well as case management

We believe the peer assistance model described above offers the best hope of resolving the problems of utilization and continuance, in that PAPs are well positioned to incorporate the features highlighted by Bartels et al. First, existing work-based assistance programs, including EAPs and PAPs, are a potent arena within which older employees can be helped to prepare for the stresses and strains that are likely to accompany retirement and to strengthen the skills they will need to cope with these stresses before they face them. Second, these programs can be modified to create retirement assistance programs aimed specifically at helping troubled retirees from a particular occupation or organization. Such programs might originate with existing retiree organizations (as in the case of the Bluebills in Washington state), or they might start off as retirement arms of existing work-based PAPs. Either way, such programs may play a key role in ensuring that retirees are able to access treatment services in a timely manner and that they follow through with whatever treatment program they initiate.

NOTES

1. The acronym *CAGE* (Ewing, 1984) stands for Cut down, Annoyed, Guilty, Eye-opener. Other commonly used screening tools include the MAST (Michigan Alcohol Screening Test; Selzer, 1971) and the AUDIT (Alcohol Use Disorders Identification Test; Saunders, Aasland, Babor, de la Fuente, & Grant, 1993). Cherpitel (1997) and Connors and Volk (2004) discuss some of the tools available and the differences between them.
2. Screening for drug abuse or misuse in an older population is more difficult than screening for drinking problems, in part because older people may be particularly sensitive to questions about illicit drug use or illegal activity relating to drug use, as we described in chapter 6. In focus groups we conducted, several participants posited that some older respondents would be so offended by the inclusion of such questions that they would likely refuse to complete the questionnaire.
3. See http://www.e-aa.org/links/links.php?ID=12 for a list of occupational AA groups.

CHAPTER 8

Conclusion and Directions for Future Research

Going to work made me an alcoholic. I can't blame [my employer] for my alcoholism. But I drank to cover up my aches and pains from work. Right now I have a bad back, a bad leg, neck and shoulders.... [Now, my friends are] proud of me [for getting sober]. I am proud of me.

—Ken, a retired autoworker

I still average about two drinks a day. I tell the doctors how much I'm drinking when they ask, and they want me to stay away from it, because of the medications. So I have to moderate it. So I moderate it in accordance with their wishes.... I can stay within my two drinks a day. That's okay.

—Ray, a retired autoworker

Ray and Ken are among the 1,300 or so retirees we studied as part of our extended research on the relationship between retirement and drinking. More broadly, they are two of the millions of Americans who either retired or became eligible for retirement over recent years.

The following recent statistics from the US Administration on Aging (2011, p. 1) are arresting:

- The older population (65+) numbered 40.4 million in 2010, an increase of 5.4 million or 15.3% since 2000.
- The number of Americans aged 45-64—who will reach 65 over the next two decades—increased by 31% during this decade.

- Over one in every eight people, or 13.1% of the population, is currently an older American.
- Persons reaching age 65 have an average life expectancy of an additional 18.8 years (20.0 years for women, 17.3 for men).
- The 85+ population is projected to increase from 5.5 million in 2010 to 6.6 million in 2020 (19% for that decade).

The United States and other Western societies are facing a demographic trend with enormous implications (Anderson, Goodman, Holtzman, Posner, & Northridge, 2012; Skirbekk, Loichinger, & Barakat, 2012). A steady rise in life spans, less procreation among 20- to 50-year-olds, and the aging of the Boomer cohort mean that as a population we are getting older. The experience of previous generations has been that older people are less prone to misuse alcohol: As we pointed out in chapter 1, by most accounts, people tend to drink less as they age (Brennan & Moos, 1990; Grant et al., 2004). But, as we have discussed, expectations based on patterns observed over previous generations may need to be revised for those now entering later life, who came of age in an era of different societal and cultural norms (National Institute on Alcohol Abuse and Alcoholism, 1998). Moreover, the new economic reality means that retirement increasingly entails an extended career in often low-end, physically challenging or painful work, with more limited retirement benefits. These trends may well combine to generate the types of conditions documented to be associated with alcohol or other substance abuse/misuse. Are we prepared for a world in which 4 million people over 65, or more—4.4 million by 2020, according to projections (Gfroerer et al., 2003)—require treatment for alcohol or substance use disorders?

We can't know the life stories of 4 million people, but we know something about a few of them. Let's look at Ken. When we interviewed him in the spring of 2000, Ken had been retired for nearly 3 years. Ken retired at 52 after 30 years on the job, mainly because he no longer liked the work; but he also emphasized that while he was working he drank a lot to help him deal with chronic back and leg pain (since retirement, he had also been diagnosed with bursitis in the neck and shoulder). At our interview, Ken claimed to have been sober for about 15 months. But leaving aside his continuing physical pain, aspects of Ken's experience suggest that he was at high risk of relapse. For instance, Ken's wife had died in 1994, leaving him alone at home. He was estranged from his adopted daughter, and while he got along with his son, the two lived in different states and did not see each other often. Ken had been diagnosed with depression and was taking medication for it. He told us that since retiring he spent most of his time alone (a situation he claimed to prefer), sleeping or watching TV, and only went out to the doctor, psychiatrist, and Alcoholics Anonymous meetings. His pets—two dachshunds, a cat, and a tank of fish—were the one thing keeping him going.

Ray, interviewed in the fall of 1999, had retired 10 years earlier at age 59, after 37 years on the job. Ray, like Ken, was in poor health; indeed, his emphysema (for which he was on supplemental oxygen) was what prompted him to retire, a step he took unwillingly. Unlike Ken, Ray had a strong social support network: While he was not especially close to his own children, he had robust, loving relationships with his second wife (who was still working) and his stepchildren. Ray said he spent his time reading, helping with household tasks, going to the library, and visiting sick friends. In keeping with his doctor's orders, Ray said he had managed to "moderate" his drinking, which he interpreted as limiting himself to two drinks a day.

If Ray and Ken's experiences reflect in any way the nature of the problem facing our society in terms of alcohol abuse and misuse among older people—and we believe that they do—then the demographic shift we are now experiencing should give us pause for thought. While few studies have specifically addressed the costs of alcohol use disorders among older adults (Bartels et al., 2005), people with untreated alcohol or drug dependence are estimated to incur health care costs at about twice the rate of their age and gender cohorts (Gerson et al., 2001; Holder, 1998). Moreover, Holder (1998), in a review of studies on the cost benefits of substance abuse treatment, found that patients aged 55 and over had the poorest prognosis and incurred the highest medical costs. In an era of limited resources, these costs will likely make treatment for those older adults who most need it less accessible, rather than more. Already, many managed care companies have reduced or even eliminated their coverage for treatment of alcohol use disorders, to keep costs down (Bartels et al., 2005). On the up side, in 2011, Medicare began offering free screening and up to four counseling sessions per year in a primary care setting for patients screening positive for alcohol misuse but who do not meet the criteria for alcohol dependence. Medicare also covers a structured assessment and brief intervention for patients who show signs of substance abuse or dependence. (See the Medicare interactive Web site at http://www.medicareinteractive.org/page2.php?topic=counselor&page=script&slide_id=925#top for complete information on Medicare coverage for the treatment and prevention of alcohol and other substance use disorders.)

The economic costs of problem drinking and alcohol use disorders among older people, expressed in increased morbidity and greater utilization of health and medical services, are but half the picture. The human costs—the effects on people like Ray and Ken and their families—are the other half.

What would Ray's life be like if he did not need his two drinks per day? In our interview, Ray said he was close to his second wife and her children but less close to his own children. This fact troubled him for a while, but "it doesn't bother me anymore. I put that away." Of course, this is only speculation on our part, but it is possible that Ray's drinking played at least some small role in distancing his children. Ken, similarly, was estranged from one of his two children (his adopted daughter). Did his drinking play a role in this family drama? Similarly, did Ken's drinking aggravate his diagnosed depression? (More on this question below.) Either way, at the time of our meeting, Ken seemed destined to spend the remainder of his life unhappy and largely alone.

As we discussed in earlier chapters, the relationship between drinking and outcomes like depression or loneliness is almost certainly not a straightforward causal one. Most likely, the true picture involves some sort of mutual feedback loop. In any case, for Ken and Ray, we have no evidence on which to base a conclusion one way or the other. Yet anyone who has known an older person with alcohol dependence or drinking problems is familiar with the tension, suffering, and heartache that these conditions can generate.

DRINKING IN THE CONTEXT OF RETIREMENT

The number of older adults suffering from alcohol or other substance use disorders is rising and stands to rise further over the coming years, with all the concomitant human and economic costs that we have discussed. Still, the vast majority of older people are not expected to develop drinking problems or substance use disorders. This statement reflects both the limits of our knowledge and an opportunity to overcome those limits. Put differently, the problem is easily stated in the aggregate, in terms of percentages across the population, but difficult to define in relation to particulars, the specific sets of people who are at risk. To bring the numbers down—to resolve the problem in the aggregate—we need first to understand the problem in terms of its particulars. Until then, any interventions we design are only stabs in the dark.

In this endeavor, the research community began with the logical first step: testing for direct effects of particular variables—chronic or acute stressors, demographic variables, aspects of life history, and so on—on alcohol misuse or drinking problems. (We will limit our remarks here to alcohol and drinking for the sake of simplicity.) Retirement is one variable that has been examined extensively for such direct effects. Yet, as we saw in chapter 3, the evidence for a direct effect of retirement on drinking behavior has been mixed, with some studies finding a positive effect, some a negative effect, and some a null effect. There are a number of reasonable explanations for these inconsistent findings, but the most important seems to be that retirement influences drinking behavior for some people but not others and in different ways for different people. In other words, retirement matters but only though its interactions with other environmental factors and individual attributes. Identifying and testing for such interactions has been the focus of our own research at the Smithers Institute, as well as studies by our fellow researchers in other institutions.

In our own work, we have looked at how a number of work-related and retirement-related factors might interact with other variables to raise the risk that retirement might contribute to risky or problematic drinking. In one study, described in chapter 4 (Bacharach, Bamberger, Biron, & Horowitz-Rozen, 2008), we found that retirement agency interacts with job satisfaction to affect drinking behavior, such that respondents who felt they had been pushed into retirement drank more than those who retired willingly and that greater job satisfaction amplified this association. In another study described in that chapter (Bacharach et al., 2007), we found that among retirees with a history of drinking problems, disengagement from work-based social networks was associated with a reduction in the severity of drinking problems. A third study discussed in chapter 4 (Nahum-Shani et al., 2013) adds to the picture produced by these findings, with evidence that the stress climate and drinking norms of a particular employee's work unit together moderate the influence of retirement on drinking behavior. Finally, in chapter 5, we further enlarged the picture by bringing in the impact of stressors that commonly arise in the context of retirement (namely, financial and marital stress) and the potential mediating role of poor sleep quality in linking retirement-related stress and drinking, especially among men (Belogolovsky et al., 2012).

In general, our work and that of others is beginning to delineate the circumstances under which retirement is more likely to precipitate or exacerbate alcohol misuse or problem drinking. For instance, a person who enjoyed his or her work, who felt forced to retire, and who is concerned about making do on a limited budget is highly at risk for alcohol misuse or problem drinking. However, if the person had been working in an environment with highly permissive drinking norms, that individual's drinking might actually decline in retirement.

WHERE DO WE GO FROM HERE?

Of course, the questions yet to be answered are legion. Looking merely at the relationships described in the last paragraph, no study has yet examined the interaction between permissive drinking norms, retirement agency, and pre-/postretirement affective states such as job stress and financial or marital strain. Other questions also present themselves. For instance, do a spouse's work status, job satisfaction, and stress levels affect the other spouse's drinking behavior in retirement? Does this differ for men and women? Consider Ray, whose wife was still working at the time of our interview. If Ray's wife were around during the day, would she be able to keep him below two drinks a day, as posited by social control theory?

Here, we will highlight several areas where the data raise additional questions, suggest alternative interpretations, or open up avenues for further research. Following that, we will consider how at least some of these issues might benefit from consideration through the lens of a theoretical perspective not yet mentioned in this volume: namely, person–environment fit.

Cohort Issues

It is clear that the coming decades will see increased substance use among retirees and bridge employees as more Baby Boomers reach retirement age. As we have discussed, while rates of alcohol consumption traditionally fall in later life, the Boomer generation is expected to break this pattern, at least in part because this generation is thought to have internalized more permissive norms about drinking and drug use during their transition into adulthood (National Institute on Alcohol Abuse and Alcoholism, 1998; Reardon, 2012). Less clear is what we can expect after that. Is the Baby Boom retirement likely to be a bubble?

Little research has been conducted on cohort differences in alcohol consumption over time (i.e., as individuals age). And we are unaware of any research examining this issue over more recent cohorts (Boomers, Gen X'ers, and Millennials). However, at least one study (Moore et al., 2005) indicates that rates of decline in consumption by age fell from early 20th-century birth cohorts to mid-century cohorts. That is, while overall there continued to be a decline in drinking with increasing age, this decline was less steep for the most recent cohort (with a mean birth year of 1945) than for the previous cohort (mean birth year 1925), which in turn saw a less steep decline than the cohort before that (mean birth year 1905). Moore et al. (2005) speculate that this trend may reflect improvements in the health of older adults over time, with earlier cohorts drinking comparatively less as they aged because of their poorer health overall. If so, this suggests that today's youngest cohorts are unlikely to return to pre-Boomer patterns with aging, meaning that a comparatively high proportion of older people will continue to be vulnerable to alcohol-related health risks well into the 21st century.

Retirement Trajectories

Another area that calls for further study is the effect of different retirement trajectories. Bridge employment versus full retirement is the most obvious distinction, but more subtle analyses are possible. Questions to consider include the following: Is the bridge job in the individual's career field or a completely different area? Is the bridge job experienced as a continuation of the career job or as disconnected from it? Is the bridge employee working because he or she needs to or because he or she wants to? And what about multigenerational effects, such as the impact of working a bridge job (or, for that matter, the impact of deferring one's retirement) in a largely younger versus older or mixed-age environment?

In general, as we pointed out in chapter 1, bridge retirement is associated with health benefits, not risks, and is better for mental health than simply deferring retirement and continuing to work (Zhan et al., 2009). However, Zhan et al. found mental health benefits for bridge employment only in the person's career field. In addition, Zhan et al. point out that their results may underestimate the physical health risks associated with bridge employment—a function of data limitations that enabled them to measure health outcomes only as dichotomous variables (i.e., the presence or absence of particular diseases or functional limitations). Furthermore, the impact of bridge employment may change over time, particularly if bridge employees are forced to continue working for financial reasons. In such cases, the apparent health benefits of bridge employment may begin to turn into risks as employees age.

An additional consideration is that financial pressures might lead older workers (particularly bridge employees) to take jobs that, in the past, they might never have considered, such as minimum-wage jobs at Walmart or McDonald's. Aside from the physical hardships involved in such jobs, there may be emotional hardships as well, stemming from the status inconsistency of either working for a manager who is much younger in age or doing menial labor despite years of education and experience. It has long been known that status inconsistency—that is, a discrepancy between an individual's position on one status hierarchy, such as that associated with age or education, and on another, such as the organizational pecking order—can be a source of stress (Bacharach, Bamberger, & Mundell, 1993). Status inconsistency can thus become an additional risk factor for drinking as a coping mechanism.

The Potential Role of Mental Illness

The well-established relationship between substance misuse and mental illness raises further questions (Bartels et al., 2005). Epidemiological studies have shown that the lifetime prevalence of a substance use disorder among people diagnosed with a mental illness is about 29%, and the converse (i.e., the lifetime prevalence of a mental illness diagnosis among people with a substance use disorder) is about 37% (Regier et al., 1990). The rate of co-occurring substance use disorders and mental illness seems to be lower among older age groups than younger ones, possibly because of the relatively low abuse rate for substances other than alcohol among older people (Bartels et al., 2005). Yet many studies have documented high rates of co-occurring mental health and substance use disorders in specialty geriatric psychiatry clinics, affecting one-fifth to one-third of those in both inpatient and outpatient settings; the mental illness most commonly diagnosed in these cases is depression (Bartels et al., 2005; Blixen, McDougall, & Suen, 1997; Devanand, 2002; Schuckit, 1986).

The interaction between mental health issues and alcohol or substance misuse in the context of retirement thus offers a potentially fruitful arena for future research. Further, such research might profitably be conducted in light of two theoretical approaches that we discussed in chapter 2 of this volume but that have been touched upon only slightly in the literature on drinking and retirement (Kuerbis & Sacco, 2012): namely, role theory and continuity theory. Role theory proposes that the transition to retirement is likely to be easier and less stressful to the degree that the individual's sense of identity is built around goals, motivations, and values drawn from outside preretirement work roles. The idea behind continuity theory is that people seek to process periods of transition in terms of their past experiences; transitions that are not amenable to such processing are more stressful. In similar ways, these theories are built around the notion that the sense of self we humans construct from our goals, values, and experiences can be a fragile thing. Intuitively, it seems likely that where episodes of change such as retirement disturb this sometimes fragile construction, depression, stress, or other negative emotional states may result. Future research might test this proposition and examine the conditions under which depression, negative emotional states, or other affective disorders then mediate the onset or exacerbation of drinking problems.

The Impact of Substance Misuse on Retirement Decision Making

Throughout this volume, we have been working on the assumption that where there is a relationship between retirement-related factors and substance misuse, the direction of causation is generally from the former to the latter. But as we pointed out in several of our reports (Bacharach et al., 2004; Bacharach, Bamberger, Sonnenstuhl, & Vashdi, 2008b), in some cases substance misuse may be an antecedent of retirement, rather than the other way around. That is, it may be that those employees most likely to retire immediately on becoming eligible are precisely those with preretirement substance use problems. These individuals may retire at the first opportunity in order to lower the risk of being detected and dismissed without benefits. Indeed, in one of our analyses we found that participants who were fully retired reported significantly more drinking problems prior to retirement than did those continuing to work (Bacharach et al., 2004). Perreira and Sloan (2001) also found retirement to be associated with increased drinking most frequently among those having a preretirement history of problem drinking.

Another question is whether substance misuse might impair retirement-related decision making. Although there is no research specifically on this question, studies demonstrate that substance misuse impairs decision making in general, increasing the tendency to make more risky decisions. For instance, Bechara and Martin (2004) found that individuals who had previously been treated for substance dependence, as a group, showed below-normal levels of performance on various measures of decision making and working memory. George, Rogers, and Duka (2005) found impaired decision making even among healthy young volunteers, all of them social drinkers who were not alcohol- or drug-dependent, following acute alcohol consumption. Participants in that study who consumed a heavily alcoholic beverage showed poorer executive function and riskier decision making compared with volunteers who drank a placebo. Any impact of substance misuse on retirement decision making thus presents a potential confound for analyses of how retirement impacts substance use.

Generalizability of Our Findings

Finally, are current findings, both our own and others', generalizable to other populations? Two dimensions are relevant here: occupation and culture. In our research, we focused on individuals who had retired from traditional blue-collar jobs in manufacturing, construction, and transportation. We chose this population precisely because these occupations are known to have relatively permissive drinking norms (see our discussion of this issue in Bacharach et al., 2007). Would we come up with the same findings if we were to repeat our research with a sample of managers and professionals? What about teachers? Police officers? Ski instructors and tennis coaches? Professional athletes? We are unaware of any attempt to examine cross-occupational differences in substance use and misuse among older adults and retirees or the extent to which such differences might stem from factors other than different occupation-specific substance use norms.

The effects of national culture (as opposed to occupational culture) are also potentially confounding. Nearly all the research explored in this book relates to older adults in the United States and assumes a retirement context such as that found in the United States. Given that retirement trajectories and lifestyles vary across countries and cultures, there is a tremendous need to examine whether our findings are generalizable to other countries. For example, consider China, where the retirement age is currently 55 for women and 60 for men and 20% of the population will be age 65 or older by 2035 (Ebbers, Hagendijk, & Smorenberg, 2008). Despite the recent introduction of pension coverage for China's vast rural population, 50% of the country's retirees still lack any meaningful retirement coverage, and even those who do have coverage can currently expect a pension no greater than half the amount of their most recent wage (Ebbers et al., 2008). As a result, many of China's older adults continue to rely on their children and grandchildren for financial support, a situation that the country's one-child policy, in force for much of the population since 1979, has made increasingly untenable. In this context, one must begin by asking whether that nation's retirees can even afford to purchase alcoholic beverages.

PERSON–ENVIRONMENT FIT THEORY

Many of the issues covered in the previous chapters, as well as those raised here as avenues for further research, may benefit from consideration through the framework of person–environment fit (P-E fit) theory. The term *P-E fit* is commonly defined as the compatibility between an individual's needs and resources, on the one hand, and those of his or her environment on the other (Edwards, Caplan, & Harrison, 1998). One of the main dimensions of P-E fit is person–organization fit, broadly defined as the degree of compatibility between individuals and the organizations in which they work (Kristof, 1996). Kristof points out that this latter construct actually entails two types of compatibility: whether the two parties share fundamental characteristics (i.e., are the individual's values, goals, personality, and attitudes congruent with the organizational culture, climate, values, goals, and norms) and whether each party can supply what the other needs (i.e., do the opportunities and rewards supplied by the organization meet employees' needs and preferences, and do employees' abilities and contributions satisfy organizational demands?). In our view, both types of compatibility are subsumed in the needs–resources equation as it can be argued that, for some people, working in a climate congruent with one's own goals and values might be a psychological need.

The P-E fit approach chimes strongly with some of the issues we raise here as avenues for further research. For example, the retiree with years of experience and education taking a minimum-wage job, which we discussed under the rubric of retirement trajectories and status inconsistency, is a classic instance of poor person–environment fit.

Notably for our purposes, P-E fit theory suggests that past compatibility is not necessarily predictive of future compatibility. That is, as individuals change over time, they may become less able to draw needed resources from their environment or provide resources required by the environment (the strain of doing physically challenging work in later life offers one example). Such negative changes in person–environment fit may generate stress for the individual, either directly or by giving rise to adverse events (Edwards et al., 1998). Consistent with the tension reduction hypothesis (Conger, 1956), individuals may then use alcohol to cope with misfit-based stressors.

As noted by Van Der Vorst, Engels, Deković, Meeus, and Vermulst (2007, p. 1072), while P-E fit issues "have been a topic for debate for years in the field of developmental psychopathology, they have generally been neglected in the research on alcohol use." Research in P-E fit also tends to be complex, due to the difficulty inherent in modeling congruence or the lack thereof (Edwards, 2002) and, in particular, in modeling the impact of changing degrees of congruence over time. But there are several ways in which the literature suggests that the P-E fit framework may offer fruitful directions for study. We will highlight three.

The Cognitive Effects of Aging and Their Potential Impact on the Retirement–Substance Misuse Relationship

One of the ways in which person–environment fit may deteriorate over time is through the cognitive effects of aging, including slowed processing speed and dementia (impaired executive function, manifested by significant declines in a person's planning, thinking, and judgment). The mechanisms behind this cognitive decline—and ways to slow or forestall it—are the object of a great deal of research, some of which has focused on the possible effects of alcohol on cognition. There is abundant evidence that with the slowing metabolism which accompanies aging, long-term alcohol consumption at elevated levels (e.g., four or more drinks a day) can have adverse cognitive implications, among them insomnia and alcohol-related dementia (Gupta & Warner, 2008). Indeed, there is evidence that acute alcohol intake impairs cognitive functioning even among social drinkers, as we saw above (George et al., 2005). On the other hand, several recent studies have examined the impact of low to moderate alcohol use on cognition in older people and have found largely beneficial effects (Kim et al., 2012; Lang, Wallace, Huppert, & Melzer, 2007). Kim et al. (2012), in their review of the literature, conclude that moderate drinking seems to have a neuroprotective effect in the elderly (p. 12). However, the mechanisms underlying such effects are unclear, and the possibility remains that they are spurious, with those in better cognitive health more able to engage in social activities, some of which involve alcohol (Lang et al., 2007).

Returning to the question of interest in this volume, we are unaware of any research examining the moderating effects of cognitive decline on the relationship between retirement and substance misuse. But it appears likely that poor cognitive function might serve in different ways as both a risk factor and a protective factor. That is, cognitive decline might make some individuals more vulnerable to alcohol misuse by impairing their ability to self-regulate their drinking. In other cases, poor cognitive function might serve as a protective factor by resulting in the individual's exclusion from social activities that revolve around alcohol. The person–environment fit framework offers a useful way of thinking about these two possible paths, by including environmental considerations in the equation—in one case, the beneficial effects of withdrawal from an environment that promotes drinking; in another, the negative effects of withdrawal from an environment that might offer a form of social control.

The Physical Effects of Aging and Their Potential Impact on the Retirement–Substance Misuse Relationship

We have discussed in several contexts how the physical effects of aging (e.g., back problems or arthritis) may either amplify or attenuate the impact of retirement or bridge employment on alcohol misuse. Alcohol is undoubtedly often used as a means of relieving pain, though medication taken for pain or other health conditions may reduce the risk of alcohol misuse as most medications list alcohol as contraindicated (Brennan, Schutte, & Moos, 2005, 2010). Whether the tendency to use alcohol for pain relief is greater among retirees versus those deferring retirement or among those who disengage from work versus those who take bridge jobs is a complex question. Certainly, those older adults engaged in physical labor, such as lifting or manual manipulation, may suffer a greater prevalence of muscle, back, and joint pain. On the other hand, awareness of such pain may be weaker among those employed and more engaged. As we saw with the cognitive aspect of aging, P-E fit theory offers a fruitful approach to such questions by broadening the issue beyond the mere presence of pain to the environment in which the individual operates.

We should mention the potential moderating role of sleep disorders in relation to the physical effects of aging. In chapter 5, we discussed our findings among older retirees who used alcohol as a means of self-medicating sleep disorders. That study focused particularly on sleep problems arising from financial and marital stressors in retirement. But many older people experience changes in their sleep patterns even in the absence of such stressors. In addition, chronic pain can give rise to insomnia or disturbed sleep, which the individual may then seek to self-medicate through alcohol use.

Unconventional Forms of Motivation for Substance Misuse

In this book, we have emphasized two sets of motivations for misusing alcohol or drugs, based on the stress and coping approach (drinking to cope with strain) and the social network approach (drinking to fit in with a social network characterized by permissive drinking norms). But the person–environment fit framework suggests that other forms of motivation may be at work in some cases. For example, for some older adults, drinking may be driven by performance issues, as when an older salesperson drinks with clients in an effort to retain them in the face of a shifting competitive environment, or to compensate for possible performance limitations in other respects.

In a recent study of work-based drinking in China (Liu, Wang, Bamberger, Shi, & Bacharach, in press), we discuss performance motivations to drink among young newcomers. Specifically, we posited and found that alcohol use norms among veteran peers and, more importantly, clients provide a basis upon which newcomers develop an understanding of how alcohol may be used to enhance job performance. Logic suggests that a similar mechanism may apply to older workers and bridge retirees, who may use drinking as a means to retain client relationships. One can easily imagine clients cajoling older salespeople into holding their talks over drinks—and paying for them!

A FEW LAST WORDS

I plan to stay on for another year until I'm 68. I'm already losing money on the deal, but it keeps me healthy. Certainly better than sitting at home and watching TV or sleeping. I hate sleeping. I kinda fear retirement. I gotta stay active to stay healthy. Even when I do retire, I'll look for part-time work. Work itself is a great wellness program.
—*Russell, a subway train conductor (aged 67)*

When I'm at work, I'm occupied. When I get home, I start to worry again. I think too much and do too little. It ain't healthy. I like the work environment. Me and the guys argue and holler at each other, but by the end of the day, we're buddies again. If I leave that, I don't know what would happen to me.
—*Salvatore (Sal), a transit authority yard worker (aged 77)*

In the Western world, we have grown used to thinking of retirement as a natural stage of life. We forget that retirement, as a concept, is not that old. In the United States, the contemporary notion of retirement came into being less than a century ago, with passage of the Social Security Act of 1935 (Atchley, 1982). The purpose of this legislation (and similar laws in other Western nations) was partly to alleviate poverty and suffering in old age but also to reduce unemployment by removing older, less productive employees from the workforce and making room for young workers with families to support. Prior to that time, most people either stayed on the job until they died or continued working until they were physically unable to do so, at which point they relied for support on their family, friends, and communities (Atchley, 1982). So today's understanding of retirement, with all its physical, social, financial, and emotional implications, is in many ways an artificial one.

Today's demographic shifts mean that we are heading in a new direction, one whose implications and outcomes are still uncertain. In some ways, the new retirement—what we have been calling bridge retirement or bridge employment—resembles the old, pre-1935 template, especially for those retirees who return to work out of financial necessity. Yet for workers like Russell and Sal, work offers social, physical, and psychological benefits that will make their later years richer and more fulfilling.

In this volume, we have tried to show that retirement—treated (1) as a complex, multifaceted variable and (2) in relation to other conditions and attributes—can be usefully examined for its potential contributing role to alcohol or other substance misuse during later life. We have, we hope, shown both why this enterprise is not straightforward and why it is nonetheless worth doing. We hope this book will inspire other (younger!) researchers to conduct etiological research of their own that will further advance our understanding of this important issue.

We also hope that this book will inspire prevention- and treatment-oriented research that builds on what we have already learned. While good evidence on pharmacological and psychotherapeutic interventions for substance abuse problems in older adults is beginning to emerge, there is an urgent need for high-quality scientific evaluation of promising prevention and treatment programs (Bartels et al., 2005; Schonfeld et al., 2010). In particular, as more and more adults defer full retirement and remain in the workforce, it is important to improve our understanding of how existing workplace prevention and treatment frameworks such as employee assistance programs and peer assistance programs may better address the special needs of this population.

Finally, we hope that this book will increase the awareness of managers, labor leaders, physicians, mental health specialists, and policy makers of the pressing need to address the problem of substance misuse in aging populations, as well as all of the complexities likely to be involved in this undertaking. Although we highlighted a myriad set of mediating, moderating, and confounding factors, our hope is that, rather than confusing the issue for these stakeholders, we have enlightened them as to the complexities inherent in addressing substance misuse in general, and among older adults in particular.

APPENDIX

The following papers are among those that have been published or prepared on the basis of our longitudinal prospective study on retirement and alcohol use in blue-collar workers. The papers are listed in order of publication.

Bacharach, S., Bamberger, P., Sonnenstuhl, W., & Vashdi, D. (2004). Retirement, risky alcohol consumption and drinking problems among blue-collar workers. *Journal of Studies on Alcohol*, 65(4), 537–545.

Bamberger, P., Sonnenstuhl, W., & Vashdi, D. (2006). Screening older, blue-collar workers for drinking problems: An assessment of the efficacy of the Drinking Problems Index. *Journal of Occupational Health Psychology*, 11(1), 119–134.

Bacharach, S., Bamberger, P., Cohen, A., & Doveh, E. (2007). Retirement, social support and drinking behavior: A cohort analysis of males with a baseline history of problem drinking. *Journal of Drug Issues*, 37(3), 525–548.

Bacharach, S., Bamberger, P., Biron, M., & Horowitz-Rozen, M. (2008). Perceived agency in retirement on retiree drinking behavior: The moderating effects of pre-retirement job satisfaction [Electronic version]. *Journal of Vocational Behavior*, 73(3), 376–386.

Bacharach, S., Bamberger, P., Sonnenstuhl, W., & Vashdi, D. (2008a). Aging and drinking problems among mature adults: The moderating effects of positive alcohol expectancies and workforce disengagement. *Journal of Studies on Alcohol and Drugs*, 69(1), 151–159.

Bacharach, S., Bamberger, P., Sonnenstuhl, W., & Vashdi, D. (2008b). Retirement and drug abuse: The conditioning role of age and retirement trajectory [Electronic version]. *Addictive Behaviors*, 33, 1610–1614.

Belogolovsky, E., Bamberger, P., & Bacharach, S. (2012). Stressors and retiree alcohol misuse: The mediating effects of sleep problems and the moderating effects of gender. *Human Relations*, 65, 705–728.

Nahum-Shani, I., Bamberger, P., & Bacharach, S. (2013). Explaining the varying effects of retirement on alcohol consumption: The role of unit-level drinking norms and stress climate. New York: Cornell University Working Paper.

REFERENCES

Adams, W. L. (1996). Alcohol use in retirement communities. *Journal of the American Geriatrics Society, 44*, 1082–1085.

Adams, W. L. (2002). The effects of alcohol on medical illnesses and medication interactions. In A. M. Gurnack, R. Atkinson, & N. J. Osgood (Eds.), *Treating alcohol and drug abuse in the elderly* (pp. 32–49). New York: Springer.

Administration on Aging. (2011). *A profile of older Americans: 2011.* US Department of Health and Human Services. Retrieved from http://www.aoa.gov/Aging_Statistics/Profile/2011/docs/2011profile.pdf

Alcoholics Anonymous. (n.d.) Seniors in sobriety (SIS): A history. Retrieved on January 18, 2013, from http://www.seniorsinsobriety.org/history.htm

American Geriatrics Society. (2008, September 5). Alcohol use disorders in older adults. *Annals of long-term care: Clinical care and aging.* Retrieved from http://www.annalsoflongtermcare.com/article/5143

American Heart Association. (2011, March). Alcoholic beverages and cardiovascular disease. Retrieved from http://www.heart.org/HEARTORG/GettingHealthy/NutritionCenter/Alcoholic-Beverages-and-Cardiovascular-Disease_UCM_305864_Article.jsp

American Psychiatric Association. (1994). Diagnostic and Statistical Manual of Mental Disorders (4th ed.) Washington, DC: Author.

American Psychiatric Association. (2013). *Diagnostic and Statistical Manual of Mental Disorders* (5th ed.) Washington, DC: Author.

Ancoli-Israel, S., & Roth, T. (1999). Characteristics of insomnia in the United States: Results of the 1991 national sleep foundation survey. I. *Sleep, 22*(Suppl. 2), S347–S353.

Anderson, L. A., Goodman, R. A., Holtzman, D., Posner, S. F., & Northridge, M. E. (2012). Aging in the United States: Opportunities and challenges for public health. *American Journal of Public Health, 102*(3), 393–395.

Arias, E. (2011). *United States life tables, 2007.* National Vital Statistics Reports (Vol. 59, No. 9). Hyattsville, MD: National Center for Health Statistics. Retrieved from www.cdc.gov/nchs/data/nvsr/nvsr59/nvsr59_09.pdf

Atchley, R. C. (1982). Retirement as a social institution. *Annual Review of Sociology, 8*, 263–287.

Atchley, R. C. (1989). A continuity theory of normal aging. *Gerontologist, 29*(2), 183–190.

Atkinson, R. M., & Misra, S. (2002). Further strategies in the treatment of aging alcoholics. In A. M. Gurnack, R. Atkinson, & N. J. Osgood (Eds.), *Treating alcohol and drug abuse in the elderly* (pp. 109–130). New York: Springer.

Atkinson, R. M., Tolson, R. L., & Turner, J. A. (1990). Late versus early onset problem drinking in older men. *Alcoholism, Clinical and Experimental Research, 14*, 574–579.

Bacharach, S., Bamberger, P., Biron, M., & Horowitz-Rozen, M. (2008). Perceived agency in retirement on retiree drinking behavior: The moderating effects of pre-retirement job satisfaction [Electronic version]. *Journal of Vocational Behavior, 73*(3), 376–386.

Bacharach, S., Bamberger, P., Cohen, A., & Doveh, E. (2007). Retirement, social support and drinking behavior: A cohort analysis of males with a baseline history of problem drinking. *Journal of Drug Issues, 37*(3), 525–548.

Bacharach, S., Bamberger, P., & Mundell, B. (1993). Status inconsistency in organizations: From social hierarchy to stress. *Journal of Organizational Behavior, 14*, 21–36.

Bacharach, S., Bamberger, P., & Sonnenstuhl, W. (2001). *Mutual aid and union renewal: Cycles of logics of action.* Ithaca, NY: Cornell University Press.

Bacharach, S., Bamberger, P., & Sonnenstuhl, W. (2002). Driven to drink: Managerial control, work-related risk factors, and employee problem drinking. *Academy of Management Journal, 45*(4), 637–658.

Bacharach, S., Bamberger, P., Sonnenstuhl, W., & Vashdi, D. (2004). Retirement, risky alcohol consumption and drinking problems among blue-collar workers. *Journal of Studies on Alcohol, 65*(4), 537–545.

Bacharach, S., Bamberger, P., Sonnenstuhl, W., & Vashdi, D. (2008a). Aging and drinking problems among mature adults: The moderating effects of positive alcohol expectancies and workforce disengagement. *Journal of Studies on Alcohol and Drugs, 69*(1), 151–159.

Bacharach, S., Bamberger, P., Sonnenstuhl, W., & Vashdi, D. (2008b). Retirement and drug abuse: The conditioning role of age and retirement trajectory [Electronic version]. *Addictive Behaviors, 33*, 1610–1614.

Bamberger, P., Sonnenstuhl, W., & Vashdi, D. (2006). Screening older, blue-collar workers for drinking problems: An assessment of the efficacy of the Drinking Problems Index. *Journal of Occupational Health Psychology, 11*(1), 119–134.

Barnas, C., Rossmann, M., Roessler, H., Reimer, Y., & Fleischhacker, W. W. (1992). Benzodiazepine and other psychotropic drug abuse by patients in a methadone maintenance program: Familiarity and preference. *Journal of Clinical Psychopharmacology, 12*, 397–402.

Barrick, C., & Connors, G. J. (2002). Relapse prevention and maintaining abstinence in older adults with alcohol-use disorders. *Drugs & Aging, 19*(8), 583–594.

Barry, K. L., Oslin, D. W., & Blow, F. C. (2001). *Alcohol problems in older adults.* New York: Springer.

Bartels, S. J., Blow, F. C., Brockmann, L. M., & Van Citters, A. D. (2005). *Substance abuse and mental health among older Americans: The state of the knowledge and future directions.* Rockville, MD: Substance Abuse and Mental Health Services Administration, Older American Substance Abuse and Mental Health Technical Assistance Center.

Basca, B. (2008). *The elderly and prescription drug misuse and abuse.* Santa Rosa, CA: Center for Applied Research Solutions.

Bechara, A., & Martin, E. M. (2004). Impaired decision making related to working memory deficits in individuals with substance addictions. *Neuropsychology, 18*(1), 152–162.

Beehr, T. A. (1986). The process of retirement: A review and recommendations for future investigation. *Personnel Psychology, 39*, 31–55.

Belogolovsky, E., Bamberger, P., & Bacharach, S. (2012). Stressors and retiree alcohol misuse: The mediating effects of sleep problems and the moderating effects of gender. *Human Relations*, *65*, 705–728.

Blazer, D. G., & Wu, L. T. (2009a). The epidemiology of at-risk and binge drinking among middle-aged and elderly community adults: National Survey on Drug Use and Health. *American Journal of Psychiatry*, *166*, 1162–1169.

Blazer, D. G., & Wu, L. T. (2009b). The epidemiology of substance use and disorders among middle-aged and elderly community adults: National Survey on Drug Use and Health. *American Journal of Geriatric Psychiatry*, *17*, 237–245.

Blazer, D. G., & Wu, L. T. (2009c). Nonprescription use of pain relievers by middle-aged and elderly community-living adults: National Survey on Drug Use and Health. *Journal of the American Geriatrics Society*, *57*, 1252–1257.

Blixen, C. E., McDougall, G. J., & Suen, L. (1997). Dual diagnosis in elders discharged from a psychiatric hospital. *International Journal of Geriatric Psychiatry*, *12*(3), 307–313.

Blow, F. T. (1998). *TIP 26: Substance abuse among older adults*. Rockville, MD: National Library of Medicine.

Brennan, P. L., & Moos, R. H. (1990). Life stressors, social resources, and late-life problem drinking. *Psychology and Aging*, *5*, 491–501.

Brennan, P. L., Schutte, K. K., & Moos, R. H. (1999). Reciprocal relations between stressors and drinking behavior: A three-wave panel study of late middle-aged and older women and men. *Addiction*, *94*, 737–749.

Brennan, P. L., Schutte, K. K., & Moos, R. H. (2005). Pain and use of alcohol to manage pain: Prevalence and 3-year outcomes among older problem and non-problem drinkers. *Addiction*, *100*, 777–786.

Brennan, P. L., Schutte, K. K., & Moos, R. H. (2010). Retired status and older adults' 10-year drinking trajectories. *Journal of Studies on Alcohol and Drugs*, *71*, 165–168.

Brennan, P. L., Schutte, K. K., SooHoo, S., & Moos, R. H. (2011). Painful medical conditions and alcohol use: A prospective study among older adults. *Pain Medicine*, *12*, 1049–1059.

Breslow, R., Faden, V., & Smothers, B. (2003). Alcohol consumption by elderly Americans. *Journal of Studies on Alcohol*, *11*, 884–892.

Brown, S. K. (2003). *Staying ahead of the curve 2003: The AARP working in retirement study*. Washington, DC: American Association of Retired Persons. Retrieved from http://assets.aarp.org/rgcenter/econ/multiwork_2003.pdf

Bullers, S., Cooper, M. L., & Russell, M. (2001). Social network drinking and adult alcohol involvement: A longitudinal exploration of the direction of influence. *Addictive Behaviors*, *26*, 181–199.

Buysse, D. J., Reynolds, C. F., III, Monk, T. H., Berman, S. R., & Kupfer, D. J. (1989). The Pittsburgh Sleep Quality Index: A new instrument for psychiatric practice and research. *Psychiatry Research*, *28*(2), 193–213.

Cahill, K. E., Giandrea, M. D., & Quinn, J. F. (2006). Retirement patterns from career employment. *The Gerontologist*, *46*(4), 514–523.

Cahill, K. E., Giandrea, M. D., & Quinn, J. F. (2007). Down shifting: The role of bridge jobs after career employment. Issue Brief 06. Boston College: Sloan Center on Aging and Work.

Cahill, K. E., Giandrea, M. D., & Quinn, J. F. (2012). Bridge employment. In M. Wang (Ed.), *Oxford handbook of retirement* (pp. 293–310). New York: Oxford University Press.

Canabou, C. (2002, April). Gone but not forgotten. *Fast Company*. Retrieved from http://www.fastcompany.com/44748/gone-not-forgotten

Center for Substance Abuse Treatment, Substance Abuse and Mental Health Services Administration. (1998). Treatment Improvement Protocol (TIP) #26: Substance abuse among older adults. Rockville, MD: Author.

Centers for Disease Control and Prevention. (2012, October). Fact Sheets—Excessive alcohol use and risks to men's health. *Alcohol and Public Health*. Retrieved from http://www.cdc.gov/alcohol/fact-sheets/mens-health.htm

Cherpitel, C. J. (1997). Brief screening instruments for alcoholism. *Alcohol Health and Research World, 21*, 348–351.

Cohn, D., & Taylor, P. (2010, December 20). Baby boomers approach age 65—Glumly. *Pew Research Social & Demographic Trends*. Retrieved from http://pewresearch.org/pubs/1834/baby-boomers-old-age-downbeat-pessimism

Conger, J. J. (1956). Alcoholism: Theory, problem and challenge. II. Reinforcement theory and the dynamics of alcoholism. *Journal of Studies on Alcohol, 13*, 296–305.

Connors, G. J., & Volk, R. J. (2004). Self-report screening for alcohol problems among adults. Retrieved from http://pubs.niaaa.nih.gov/publications/AssessingAlcohol/selfreport.htm

Cooper, M. L. (1994). Motivations for alcohol use among adolescents: Development and validation of a four-factor model. *Psychological Assessment, 6*, 117–128.

Cooper, M. L., Russell, M., Skinner, J. B., Frone, M. R., & Mudar, P. (1992). Stress and alcohol use: Moderating effects of gender, coping, and alcohol expectancies. *Journal of Abnormal Psychology, 101*, 139–152.

Cox, W. M., & Klinger, E. (1988). A motivational model of alcohol use. *Journal of Abnormal Psychology, 97*, 168–180.

Cronkite, R., & Moos, R. (1984). The role of predisposing and moderating factors in the stress–illness relationship. *Journal of Health and Social Behavior, 25*, 372–393.

Cunningham, J. A., Wild, T. C., Cordingley, J., van Mierlo, T., & Humphreys, K. (2009). A randomized controlled trial of an Internet-based intervention for alcohol abusers. *Addiction, 104*(12), 2023–2032.

Devanand, D. P. (2002). Comorbid psychiatric disorders in late life depression. *Biological Psychiatry, 52*(3), 236–242.

Dew, J., & Yorgason, J. (2010). Economic pressure and marital conflict in retirement-aged couples. *Journal of Family Issues, 31*(2), 164–188.

Dufour, M., & Fuller, R. K. (1995). Alcohol in the elderly. *Annual Review of Medicine, 46*, 123–132.

Duhigg, C. (2012). *The power of habit*. New York: Random House.

Ebbers, H., Hagendijk, R., & Smorenberg, H. (2008). China's pension system. Mn Services and Nyenrode Business Universiteit. Retrieved from http://www.mn.nl/pls/portal/docs/PAGE/MN_CORPORATE_2011/CONTENT_MN/PDF_BIJLAGEN/PAPERS_EN_RAPPORTEN/POSITION%20PAPER%20CHINA%27S%20PENSION%20SYSTEM.PDF

Edwards, J. R. (2002). Alternatives to difference scores: Polynomial regression analysis and response surface methodology. In F. Drasgow & N. W. Schmitt (Eds.), *Advances in measurement and data analysis* (pp. 350–400). San Francisco: Jossey-Bass.

Edwards, J. R., Caplan, R. D., & Harrison, R. V. (1998). Person–environment fit theory: Conceptual foundations, empirical evidence, and directions for future research. In C. L. Cooper (Ed.), *Theories of organizational stress* (pp. 28–67). Oxford: Oxford University Press.

Ekerdt, D. J., De Labry, L. O., Glynn, R. J., & Davis, R. W. (1989). Change in drinking behaviors with retirement: Findings from the normative aging study. *Journal of Studies on Alcohol, 50*(4), 347–353.

Ewing, J. A. (1984). Detecting alcoholism: The CAGE questionnaire. *Journal of the American Medical Association, 252*, 1905–1907.

Falkin, G. P., & Strauss, S. M. (2003). Social supports and drug use enablers: A dilemma for women in recovery. *Addictive Behaviors, 28*(1), 141–155.

Finney, J. W., Moos, R. H., & Brennan, P. L. (1991). The Drinking Problems Index: A measure to assess alcohol-related problems among older adults. *Journal of Substance Abuse, 3*, 395–404.

Fleming, M. (2002). Identification and treatment of alcohol use disorders in older adults. In A. M. Gurnack, R. Atkinson, & N. J. Osgood (Eds.), *Treating alcohol and drug abuse in the elderly* (pp. 85–108). New York: Springer.

Fleming, M. F., Barry, K. L., Manwell, L. B., Johnson, K., & London, R. (1997). Brief physician advice for problem alcohol drinkers: A randomized controlled trial in community-based primary care practices. *Journal of the American Medical Association, 277*, 1039–1045.

Fleming, M. F., Manwell, L. B., Barry, K. L., Adams, W., & Stauffacher, E. A. (1999). Brief physician advice for alcohol problems in older adults: A randomized community-based trial. *Journal of Family Practice, 48*(5), 378–384.

Fromme, K., Stroot, E. A., & Kaplan, D. (1993). Comprehensive effects of alcohol: Development and psychometric assessment of a new expectancy questionnaire. *Psychological Assessment, 5*, 19–26.

Frone, M. R. (1999). Work stress and alcohol use. *Alcohol Research & Health, 23*, 284–291.

Frone, M. R. (2013). *Alcohol and illicit drug use in the workplace and the workforce.* Washington, DC: American Psychological Association.

Gallo, W. T. (2012). The association of retirement with physical and behavioral health. In M. Wang (Ed.), *The Oxford handbook of retirement.* New York: Oxford University Press.

George, L. K. (1993). Sociological perspectives on life transitions. *Annual Review of Sociology, 19*, 353–373.

George, S., Rogers, R. D., & Duka, T. (2005). The acute effect of alcohol on decision making in social drinkers. *Psychopharmacology, 182*, 160–169.

Gerson, L. W., Boex, J., Hua, K., Liebelt, R. A., Zumbar, W. R., Bush, D., et al. (2001). Medical care use by treated and untreated substance abusing Medicaid patients. *Journal of Substance Abuse Treatment, 20*(2), 115–120.

Gfroerer, J., Penne, M., Pemberton, M., & Folsom, R. (2003). Substance abuse treatment need among older adults in 2020: The impact of the aging baby-boom cohort. *Drug and Alcohol Dependence, 69*, 127–135.

Golan, M., & Bamberger, P. (2009). The cross-cultural transferability of a peer-based employee assistance program (EAP): A case study. *Journal of Workplace Behavioral Health, 24*, 399–418.

Goldman, M. S. (1994). The alcohol expectancy concept: Applications to assessment, prevention, and treatment of alcohol abuse. *Applied & Preventive Psychology, 3*, 131–144.

Grant, B. F., Dawson, D. A., Stinson, F. S., Chou, S. P., Dufour, M. C., & Pickering, R. P. (2004). The 12-month prevalence and trends in DSM-IV alcohol abuse and dependence: United States, 1991–1992 and 2001–2002. *Drug and Alcohol Dependence, 74*(3), 223–234.

Gruenewald, P. J., & Johnson, F. W. (2006). The stability and reliability of self-reported drinking measures. *Journal of Studies on Alcohol, 67*, 738–745.

Gruenewald, P. J., & Nephew, T. (1994). Drinking in California: Theoretical and empirical analysis of alcohol consumption patterns. *Addiction, 89*, 707–723.

Gupta, S., & Warner, J. (2008). Alcohol-related dementia: A 21st-century silent epidemic? *British Journal of Psychiatry, 193*, 351–353.

Gurnack, A. M., Atkinson, R., & Osgood, N. J. (2002). *Treating alcohol and drug abuse in the elderly.* New York: Springer.

Hagihara, A., Tarumi, K., & Nobutomo, K. (2003). Positive and negative effects of social support on the relationship between work stress and alcohol consumption. *Journal of Studies on Alcohol, 64*(6), 874–883.

Han, B., Gfroerer, J., & Colliver, J. (2009, August). An examination of trends in illicit drug use among adults aged 50 to 59 in the United States. OAS Data Review. Rockville, MD: Substance Abuse and Mental Health Services Administration, Office of Applied Studies.

Harrison, J. R., & Carroll, G. (2006). *Culture and demography in organizations.* Princeton, NJ: Princeton University Press.

Hartwell, T. D., Steele, P., French, M. T., Potter, F. J., Rodman, F. N., & Zarkin, G. A. (1996). Aiding troubled employees: The prevalence, cost, and characteristics of employee assistance programs in the United States. *American Journal of Public Health, 86*, 804–808.

Hébert, B.-P., & Luong, M. (2008). Bridge employment [Electronic version]. *Perspectives on Labour and Income, 9*(11), 5–12.

Henkens, K., van Solinge, H., & Gallo, W. T. (2008). Effects of retirement voluntariness on changes in smoking, drinking and physical activity among Dutch older workers. *European Journal of Public Health, 18*, 644–649.

Hirschi, T. (2002). *Causes of delinquency.* New Brunswick, NJ: Transaction.

Hobfoll, S. E. (1988). *The ecology of stress.* Washington, DC: Hemisphere.

Hobfoll, S. E. (1989). Conservation of resources: A new attempt at conceptualizing stress. *American Psychologist, 44*(3), 513–524.

Holder, H. D. (1998). Cost benefits of substance abuse treatment: An overview of results from alcohol and drug abuse. *Journal of Mental Health Policy and Economics, 1*(1), 23–29.

Hopkins, K. M. (1997). Supervisor intervention with troubled workers: A social identity perspective. *Human Relations, 50*, 1215–1238.

Hublin, C., Partinen, M., Koskenvuo, M., & Kaprio, J. (2007). Sleep and mortality: A population-based 22-year follow-up study. *Sleep, 30*(10), 1245–1253.

Johnson, J. E. (1997). Insomnia, alcohol, and over-the-counter drug use in old-old urban women. *Journal of Community Health Nursing, 14*(3), 181–188.

Johnson, P. B., & Gurin, G. (1994). Negative affect, alcohol expectancies and alcohol-related problems. *Addiction, 89*, 581–586.

Joseph, C. L., Atkinson, R. M., & Ganzini, L. (1995). Problem drinking among residents of a VA nursing home. *International Journal of Geriatric Psychiatry, 10*, 243–248.

Kammeyer-Mueller, J., Wanberg, C., Rubenstein, A., & Song, Z. (2012). Support, undermining, and newcomer socialization: Fitting in during the first 90 days [Electronic version]. *Academy of Management Journal.*

Kennedy, G. J., Efremova, I., Frazier, A., & Saba, A. (1999). The emerging problems of alcohol and substance abuse in late life. *Journal of Social Distress and the Homeless, 8*, 227–239.

Kerr, W. C., Fillmore, K. M., & Bostrom, A. (2002). Stability of alcohol consumption over time: Evidence from three longitudinal surveys from the United States. *Journal of Studies on Alcohol, 63*, 325–333.

Kessler, R. C., Turner, J. B., & House, J. S. (1988). Effects of unemployment on health in a community survey: Main, modifying, and mediating effects. *Journal of Social Issues, 44*(4), 69–85.

Kim, J. W., Lee, D. Y., Lee, B. C., Jung, M. H., Kim, H., Choi, Y. S., et al. (2012). Alcohol and cognition in the elderly: A review. *Psychiatry Investigation, 9*(1), 8–16.

Kline, R. B. (1996). Eight-month predictive validity and covariance structure of the alcohol expectancy questionnaire for adolescents (AEQ-A) for junior high school students. *Journal of Studies on Alcohol, 57,* 396–405.

Kochanek, K. D., Xu, J. Q., Murphy, S. L., Miniño, A. M., & Kung, H. (2011, December 29). Deaths: Final data for 2009. *National Vital Statistics Reports* (Vol. 60, No. 3). Hyattsville, MD: National Center for Health Statistics. Retrieved from www.cdc. gov/nchs/data/nvsr/nvsr60/nvsr60_03.pdf

Koc-Menard, S. (2009). Knowledge transfer after retirement: The role of corporate alumni networks. *Development and Learning in Organizations, 23*(2), 9–11.

Kristof, A. L. (1996). Person–organization fit: An integrative review of its conceptualizations, measurement, and implications. *Personnel Psychology, 49*(1), 1–49.

Kuerbis, A., & Sacco, P. (2012). The impact of retirement on the drinking pattern of older adults: A review. *Addictive Behaviors, 37,* 587–595.

Kushnir, T., & Melamed, S. (1992). The Gulf War and its impact on burnout and well-being of working civilians. *Psychological Medicine, 22,* 987–995.

Landis, C. A., & Moe, K. E. (2004). Sleep and menopause. *Nursing Clinics of North America, 39*(1), 97–115.

Lang, I., Wallace, R. B., Huppert, F. A., & Melzer, D. (2007). Moderate alcohol consumption in older adults is associated with better cognition and well-being than abstinence. *Age and Ageing, 36,* 256–261.

Lee-Chiong, T. L. (2006). *Sleep: A comprehensive handbook.* Hoboken, NJ: John Wiley & Sons.

Leigh, B. C., & Stacy, A. W. (1993). Alcohol outcome expectancies: Scale construction and predictive utility in higher order confirmatory models. *Psychological Assessment, 5,* 216–229.

Leigh, B. C., & Stacy, A. W. (2004). Alcohol expectancies and drinking in different age groups. *Addiction, 99,* 215–227.

Levinson, D. J. (1986). A conception of adult development. *American Psychologist, 41,* 3–13.

Lex, B. W. (1991). Some gender differences in alcohol and polysubstance users. *Health Psychology, 10,* 121–132.

Liberto, J. G., Osline, D. W., & Ruskin, P. E. (1992). Alcoholism in older persons: A review of the literature. *Hospital & Community Psychiatry, 43,* 974–984.

Lin, X., & Leung, K. (2010). Differing effects of coping strategies on mental health during prolonged unemployment: A longitudinal analysis. *Human Relations, 63,* 637–665.

Liu, S., Wang, M., Bamberger, P., Shi, J., & Bacharach, S. B. (in press). The dark side of socialization: A longitudinal investigation of newcomer alcohol use. Academy of Management Journal.

McKee-Ryan, F. M., Song, Z., Wanberg, C. R., & Kinicki, A. J. (2005). Psychological and physical well-being during unemployment: A meta-analytic study. *Journal of Applied Psychology, 90*(1), 53–76.

Melamed, S., Shirom, A., Toker, S., Berliner, S., & Shapira, I. (2006). Burnout and risk of cardiovascular disease: Evidence, possible causal paths, and promising research directions. *Psychological Bulletin, 132*(3), 327–353.

Merrick, E. L., Hodgkin, D., Garnick, D. W., Horgan, C. M., Panas, L., Ryan, M., et al. (2008). Unhealthy drinking patterns and receipt of preventative medical services by older adults. *Journal of General Internal Medicine*, 23(11), 1741–1748.

Midanik, L. T., Soghikian, K., Ransom, L. J., & Tekawa, I. S. (1995). The effect of retirement on mental health and health behaviors: The Kaiser Permanente Retirement Study. *Journals of Gerontology Series B: Psychological Sciences and Social Sciences*, 50, S59–S61.

Moore, A. A., Gould, R., Reuben, D. B., Greendale, G. A., Carter, M. K., Zhou, K., et al. (2005). Longitudinal patterns and predictors of alcohol consumption in the United States. *American Journal of Public Health*, 95(3), 458–464.

Moore, A. A., Karno, M. P., Grella, C. E., Lin, J. C., Warda, U., Lio, D. H., et al. (2009). Alcohol, tobacco, and nonmedical drug use in older US adults: Data from the 2001/02 National Epidemiologic Survey of Alcohol and Related Conditions. *Journal of the American Geriatrics Society*, 57, 2275–2281.

Moos, R. H., Brennan, P. L., Schutte, K. K., & Moos, B. S. (2010). Older adults' health and late-life drinking patterns: A 20-year perspective. *Aging & Mental Health*, 14(1), 33–43

Moos, R. H., & Moos, B. S. (1994). *Life Stressors and Social Resources Inventory: Adult form manual*. Odessa, FL: Psychological Assessment Resources.

Moos, R. H., Schutte, K. K., Brennan, P. L., & Moos, B. S. (2009). Older adults' alcohol consumption and late-life drinking problems: A 20-year perspective. *Addiction*, 104, 1293–1302.

Moos, R. H., Schutte, K. K., Brennan P. L., & Moos, B. S. (2010). Late-life and life history predictors of older adults' high risk consumption and drinking problems. *Drug and Alcohol Dependence*, 108, 13–20.

Mundt, M. P. (2006). Analyzing the costs and benefits of brief intervention [Electronic version]. *Alcohol Research and Health*, 29(1), 34–36.

Nahum-Shani, I., Bamberger, P., Bacharach, S., & Doveh, E. (2013). Explaining the varying effects of retirement on alcohol consumption: The role of unit-level drinking norms and stress climate. New York: Cornell University Working Paper.

National Institute on Alcohol Abuse and Alcoholism. (1998). *Alcohol Alert No. 40: Alcohol and aging*. Bethesda, MD: US Department of Health and Human Services, National Institutes of Health. Retrieved from http://pubs.niaaa.nih.gov/publications/aa40.htm

National Institute on Alcohol Abuse and Alcoholism. (2000). *Tenth Special Report to the U.S. Congress on Alcohol and Health: Highlights from Current Research*. NIH Publication No. 00-1583. Bethesda, MD: Author.

Neighbors, C., Lee, C. M., Lewis, M. A., Fossos, N., & Walter, T. (2009). Internet-based personalized feedback to reduce 21st-birthday drinking: A randomized controlled trial of an event-specific prevention intervention. *Journal of Consulting and Clinical Psychology*, 77(1), 51–63.

Neve, R. J., Lemmens, P. H., & Drop, M. J. (2000). Changes in alcohol use and drinking problems in relation to role transitions in different stages of the life course. *Substance Abuse*, 21(3), 163–178.

Newton, N. C., Teesson, M., Vogl, L. E., & Andrews, G. (2010). Internet-based prevention for alcohol and cannabis use: Final results of the Climate Schools course. *Addiction*, 105(4), 749–759.

Nolen-Hoeksema, S. (2004). Gender differences in risk factors and consequences for alcohol use and problems. *Clinical Psychology Review*, 24(8), 981–1010.

Osilla, K. C., Zellmer, S. P., Larimer, M. E., Neighbors, C., & Marlatt, G. A. (2008). A brief intervention for at-risk drinking in an employee assistance program. *Journal of Studies of Alcohol and Drugs, 69,* 14–20.

Oslin, D. W. (2000). Alcohol use in late life: Disability and comorbidity. *Journal of Geriatric Psychiatry and Neurology, 13,* 134–140.

Oslin, D. W., Streim, J. E., Parmelee, P., Boyce, A. A., & Katz, I. R. (1997). Alcohol abuse: A source of reversible functional disability among residents of a VA nursing home. International Journal of Geriatric Psychiatry, *12*(8), 825–832.

Perkins, H. W. (1997). College student misperceptions of alcohol and other drug norms among peers: Exploring causes, consequences, and implications for prevention programs. In H. W. Perkins and A. Berkowitz (Eds.), *Designing alcohol and other drug prevention programs in higher education* (pp. 177–206). Newton, MA: Department of Education, Higher Education Center for Alcohol and Other Drug Prevention.

Perkins, H. W., & Berkowitz, A. D. (1986). Perceiving the community norms of alcohol use among students: Some research implications for campus alcohol education programming. *Substance Use & Misuse, 21,* 961–976.

Perreira, K. M., & Sloan, F. A. (2001). Life events and alcohol consumption among mature adults: A longitudinal analysis. *Journal of Studies on Alcohol, 62*(4), 501–508.

Perreira, K. M., & Sloan, F. A. (2002). Excess alcohol consumption and health outcomes: A 6-year follow-up of men over age 50 from the Health and Retirement Study. *Addiction, 97,* 301–310.

Pfeffer, J. (1983). Organizational demography. *Research in Organizational Behavior, 5,* 299–357.

Platt, A., Sloan, F. A., & Costanzo, P. (2010). Alcohol-consumption trajectories and associated characteristics among adults older than age 50. *Journal of Studies on Alcohol and Drugs, 71,* 169–179.

Preston, P., & Goodfellow, M. (2006). Cohort comparisons: Social learning explanations for alcohol use among adolescents and older adults. *Addictive Behaviors, 31,* 2268–2283.

Préville, M., Boyer, R., Grenier, S., Dubé, M., Voyer, P., Punti, R., et al. (2008). The epidemiology of psychiatric disorders in Quebec's older adult population. *Canadian Journal of Psychiatry, 53,* 822–832.

Price, R. H., Choi, J. N., & Vinokur, A. D. (2002). Links in the chain of adversity following job loss: How financial strain and loss of personal control lead to depression, impaired functioning, and poor health. *Journal of Occupational Health Psychology, 7*(4), 302–312.

Quan, S. F., Katz, R., Olson, J., Bonekat, W., Enright, P. L., Young, T., et al. (2005). Factors associated with incidence and persistence of symptoms of disturbed sleep in an elderly cohort: The Cardiovascular Health Study. *American Journal of the Medical Sciences, 329*(4), 163–172.

Reardon, C. (2012). The changing face of older adult substance abuse. *Social Work Today, 12*(1), 8.

Regier, D. A., Farmer, M. E., Rae, D. S., Locke, B. Z., Keith, S. J., Judd, L. L., et al. (1990). Comorbidity of mental disorders with alcohol and other drug abuse: Results from the Epidemiologic Catchment Area (ECA) study. *Journal of the American Medical Association, 264*(19), 2511–2518.

Richman, J. A., Zlatoper, K. W., Zackula Ehmke, J. L., & Rospenda, K. M. (2006). Retirement and drinking outcomes: Lingering effects of workplace stress? *Addictive Behaviors, 31,* 767–776.

Rodriguez, E., & Chandra, P. (2006). Alcohol, employment status, and social benefits: One more piece of the puzzle. *American Journal of Drug and Alcohol Abuse*, *32*(2), 237–259.

Rohsenow, D. J. (1983). Drinking habits and expectancies about alcohol's effects for self versus others. *Journal of Consulting and Clinical Psychology*, *51*, 752–756.

Roth, T. (2005). Prevalence, associated risks, and treatment patterns of insomnia. *Journal of Clinical Psychiatry*, *66*(Suppl. 9), 10–13, quiz 42–43.

Ruben, D. H. (1992). The elderly and alcohol and medication abuse. In C. E. Stout, J. L. Levitt, & D. H. Ruben (Eds.), *Handbook for assessing and treating addictive disorders* (pp. 215–235). Westport, CT: Greenwood Press.

Saunders, J. B., Aasland, O. G., Babor, T. F., de la Fuente, J. R., & Grant, M. (1993). Development of the Alcohol Use Disorders Identification Test (AUDIT): WHO Collaborative Project on Early Detection of Persons with Harmful Alcohol Consumption. II. *Addiction*, *88*, 791–804.

Schonfeld, L., & Dupree, L. W. (1995). Treatment approaches for older problem drinkers. *International Journal of the Addictions*, *30*(13–14), 1819–1842.

Schonfeld, L., & Dupree, L. W. (2002). Age-specific cognitive-behavioral and self-management treatment approaches. In A. M. Gurnack, R. Atkinson, & N. J. Osgood (Eds.), *Treating alcohol and drug abuse in the elderly* (pp. 109–130). New York: Springer.

Schonfeld, L., King-Kallimanis, B. L., Duchene, D. M., Etheridge, R. L., Herrera, J. R., Barry, K. L., et al. (2010). Screening and brief intervention for substance misuse among older adults: The Florida BRITE project. *American Journal of Public Health*, *100*(1), 108–114.

Schuckit, M. A. (1986). Genetic and clinical implications of alcoholism and affective disorder. *American Journal of Psychiatry*, *143*, 140–147.

Seeman, M., & Anderson, C. S. (1983). Alienation and alcohol: The role of work, mastery, and community in drinking behavior. *American Sociological Review*, *48*(1), 60–77.

Selzer, M. (1971). The Michigan Alcoholism Screening Test: The quest for a new diagnostic instrument. *American Journal of Psychiatry*, *127*, 1653–1658.

Shultz, K. S., Morton, K. R., & Weckerle, J. R. (1998). The influence of push and pull factors on voluntary and involuntary early retirees' retirement decision and adjustment. *Journal of Vocational Behavior*, *53*, 45–57.

Shultz, K. S., & Wang, M. (2011). Psychological perspectives on the changing nature of retirement. *American Psychologist*, *66*(3), 170–179.

Simoni-Wastila, L., & Yang, H. K. (2006). Psychoactive drug abuse in older adults. *American Journal of Geriatric Pharmacotherapy*, *4*, 380–394.

Skinner, H. A. (1982). The Drug Abuse Screening Test. *Addictive Behaviors*, *7*, 363–371.

Skirbekk, V., Loichinger, E., & Barakat, B. F. (2012). The aging of the workforce in European countries. In J. Hedge & W. C. Borman (Eds.), *The Oxford handbook of work and aging* (pp. 60–79). New York: Oxford University Press.

Smith, J. W. (1995). Medical manifestations of alcoholism in the elderly. *International Journal of Addiction*, *30*, 1749–1798.

Söderström, M., Ekstedt, M., Åkerstedt, T., Nilsson, J., & Axelsson, B. A. (2004). Sleep and sleepiness in young individuals with high burnout scores. *Sleep*, *27*, 1369–1377.

Spell, C. S., & Blum, T. C. (2005). Adoption of workplace substance abuse programs: Strategic choice and institutional perspectives. *Academy of Management Journal*, *48*, 1125–1142.

Substance Abuse and Mental Health Services Administration. (1996). *Preliminary estimates from the 1995 National Household Survey on Drug Abuse* (Advance Report No. 18, DHHS Publication No. SMA 96–3107). Rockville, MD: Author.

Substance Abuse and Mental Health Services Administration. (2000). *Summary of findings from the 1999 National Household Survey on Drug Abuse* (National Household Survey on Drug Abuse Series H-12, DHHS Publication No. SMA 00–3466). Rockville, MD: Author.

Substance Abuse and Mental Health Services Administration. (2003). Results from the 2002 National Survey on Drug Use and Health: National findings (National Household Survey on Drug Abuse Series H-22, DHHS Publication No. SMA 03–3836). Rockville, MD: Author.

Substance Abuse and Mental Health Services Administration. (2011, February 24). *The DAWN Report: Emergency department visits involving adverse reactions to medications among older adults.* Rockville, MD: Author.

Szinovacz, M. E. (2003). Context and pathways: Retirement as an institution, process, and experience. In G. A. Adams & T. A. Beehr (Eds.), *Retirement: Reasons, processes, and results* (pp. 6–52). New York: Springer.

Taylor, M. H., & Grossberg, G. T. (2012). The growing problem of illicit substance abuse in the elderly: A review [Electronic version]. *The Primary Care Companion for CNS Disorders, 14*(4).

Van der Vorst, H., Engels, R. C., Deković, M., Meeus, W., & Vermulst, A. A. (2007). Alcohol-specific rules, personality and adolescents' alcohol use: A longitudinal person–environment study. *Addiction, 102,* 1064–1075.

Vela-Bueno, A., Moreno-Jiménez, B., Rodríguez-Muñoz, A., Olavarrieta-Bernardino, S., Fernández-Mendoza, J., De la Cruz-Troca, J., et al. (2008). Insomnia and sleep quality among primary care physicians with low and high burnout levels. *Journal of Psychosomatic Research, 64*(4), 435–442.

Voyer, P., Préville, M., Roussel, M. E., Berbiche, D., & Beland, S. G. (2009). Factors associated with benzodiazepine dependence among community-dwelling seniors. *Journal of Community Health Nursing, 26*(3), 101–113.

Wang, M. (2007). Profiling retirees in the retirement transition and adjustment process: Examining the longitudinal change patterns of retirees' psychological well-being. *Journal of Applied Psychology, 92*(2), 455–474.

Wang, M., & Shultz, K. S. (2010). Employee retirement: A review and recommendations for future investigation [Electronic version]. *Journal of Management, 36,* 172.

Wang, M., Zhan, Y., Liu, S., & Shultz, K. (2008). Antecedents of bridge employment: A longitudinal investigation. *Journal of Applied Psychology, 93,* 818–830.

Werner, M. J., Walker, L. S., & Greene, J. W. (1995). Relationship of alcohol expectancies to problem drinking among college-age women. *Journal of Adolescent Health, 16,* 191–199.

Wu, L. T., & Blazer, D. G. (2011). Illicit and nonmedical drug use among older adults: A review. *Journal of Aging and Health, 23,* 481–504.

Zhan, Y., Wang, M., Liu, S., & Shultz, K. (2009). Bridge employment and retirees' health: A longitudinal investigation. *Journal of Occupational Health Psychology, 14*(4), 374–389.

INDEX

Note: Figures and tables are indicated by page numbers in italics.

health care settings
  alcohol-related problems, 2, 10–11
  cost of substance abuse, 121
  drug dependence, 91–92
  population studies ignoring, 2
health issues
  acute health events and drinking, 13
  age-related conditions for retirees,
    76–77
  at-risk and problem drinking, 1–2
  Boomer retiree attitudes, 15
  bridge employment, 125
  in brief interventions, 104–105
  challenges presented, 70
  drug abuse and early retirement, 98
  moderate alcohol use, 10
  painful medical conditions and drink-
    ing behavior, 75–76, 120–121
  physical health and drinking related,
    12–13
  physical and mental health related to
    drinking, 12–13
  reasons for retirement, 54
  younger retirees, 94
Health and Retirement Study, 35, *38*, 39,
  44, 48
heavy drinking. *See also* problem
    drinking
  definition, 5
  periodic. *See* binge drinking
  retirement decision making and, 127
Hébert, B.-P., 14
Henkens, K., *37*, 39–40, 46
Hirschi, T., 25
Hobfolls' conservation of resources
    theory, 80
Hobfoll, S. E., 80
Holder, H. D., 121
HPA axis, 80
human resource management
  alumni networks, 116–117
  intervention strategies, 100
  programs for bridge employees,
    114–115
  retirement planning, 115–116
hypertension, 101

illicit drugs, definition, 87–88
illicit drug use, 85
  alcohol use compared, 86

among older adults, 86–88, 118
criteria for dependence or abuse, 87
immediate post-Boomer cohort, 87
incidence of addiction among older
    adults, 86
Schedule 1, 88
sociodemographic factors, 93
insomnia. *See* sleep-related problems
Internet-based screening and brief inter-
    ventions, 102
intervention and counseling
  pharmaceutical therapies, 109–110
  psychosocial interventions, 101–109
  work-based assistance model,
    110–114
  workplace, 98

job satisfaction, 53
  retirement agency and, 57–60, 123

Kaiser Permanente Retirement Study,
  38, 44
  gender and protective effect of retire-
    ment, 55
Kennedy, G. J., 2, 5, 8, 9, 10, 86, 101,
  108
Kim, J. W., 130
Kristof, A. L., 129
Kuerbis, A., 1, 2, 4, 10, 11, 12, 13, 21, 22,
  24, 25, 34, 38, 39, 50, 126

labor force. *See also* bridge employment
  retiree participation in, 14
labor unions, 111, 112
Leigh, B. C., 64, 65, 66
leisure time, as retirement stressor, 21
Lemmens, P. H., 42
life course perspective, 26–27
  auto worker stories, 119, 120–121
  evaluated, 20
  model, 32, *32*
  well-being in retirement, 49
life events, 13–14
life expectancy, 1
  recent statistics, 120
life spheres, interdependence of, 26–27
long-term care, 70
loss-or-relief framework for retirees,
  22–23
  social networks, 23

part-time work after retirement. *See* bridge employment

Peer assistance programs (PAPs), 111–114
  alumni networks, 116–117
  preretirement training sessions, 115–116
  referral to, 115
  treatment improvement protocol, 117–118

peer counselors (PAPs), 112–113

PE-fit theory, 128–129
  cognitive effects of aging and retirement-substance misuse, 130
  modeling challenges, 129
  past versus future compatibility, 129
  person-organization fit, 129
  physical effects of aging and retirement-substance misuse, 131
  unconventional forms of motivation for substance misuse, 131–132

pension benefits, 14–15

periodic heavy drinking. *See* binge drinking

Perreira, K. M., 8, 13, 23, *37*, 39, 40, 42, 44, 46, 61, 127

person-environment fit (PE-fit) theory, 128–129. *See also* PE-fit theory

Pew Research Center, 15

pharmaceutical adjuncts
  averse agents, 110
  opioid receptor antagonists, 110

pharmaceutical therapies, 109–111

physiology of aging
  adverse reactions to pharmaceuticals, 88–89
  alcohol for self-medication, 131
  and alcohol use, 7–11, 59–60
  cognitive effects, 130
  symptoms of prescription drug abuse and, 91

Pittsburgh Sleep Quality Index, 82–83

Platt, A., 12, 13, *38*, 44

prescription drug disorders, 90–91
  age cohorts compared, 92
  manipulating the system, 91–92

prescription medications
  abuse/misuse, 85
  benzodiazepines, 89, *90*
  contraindications for alcohol, 131
  as drugs of abuse, 88

greatest potential for abuse/dependence (list), 89–90, *90*
  incidence of use, 88
  interactions with alcohol, 9–10, *10*, 89
  limiting interactions with alcohol, 76
  opioids, 89
  pharmaceutical adjuncts for problem drinking, 109–110
  as pyschoactive, 85
  risk of adverse reactions, 88
  screening and intervention, 106, 107
  sleep-related problems, 81

prevention and treatment programs, need for, 133

Préville, M., 91, 92

problem drinking. *See also* alcohol misuse
  baseline predictions of stressors, 74–75
  chronic stress related, 73–74
  classifying, 71
  cognitive impairment, 130
  definition, 1, 4–5, *5*
  economic costs of, 121
  increased modal consumption related, 74
  likelihood of reduced postretirement consumption, 61
  male versus female behaviors, 72–73
  methodological problems, 46
  prevalence and severity, 3
  rates among older adults, 2
  reversibility with abstinence, 101
  stressors and social resources, 72
  workplace social networks and, 60–62

Project BRITE (Brief Intervention and Treatment for Elders), 106

Project GOAL (Guiding Older Adult Lifestyles), 106

Project TrEAT (Trial for Early Alcohol Treatment), 105–106

psychoactive drug disorders
  diagnosed alcohol use disorder, 93
  risk factors, 92
  women, 93

psychoactive drugs, dependency potential, 99

psychological workload, 56, 57

psychosocial interventions, 101–109

psychotropic drugs, interactions with alcohol, 9, 89

Quinn, J. F., 14, 15

Schonfeld, L., 11, 106, 107, 108, 133
Schutte, K. K., 2, 3, 13, 25, 43, 71, 75,
　　108, 109, 131
screening
　issues with older adults, 118
　preretirement substance misuse, 115
screening for alcohol dependence,
　　102–103
　CAGE screening tool, 103–104, *103*
　Drinking Problems Index (DPI), 103
　major features, 104
self-control and role of circumstance, 25
self-identity, 22
self-reports of alcohol consumption, 40
Seniors in Sobriety movement (AA), 108
sensitivity (of screening tools), 103
sexual harassment, 56, 57
Short Michigan Alcoholism Screening
　　Instrument—Geriatric Version
　　(SMAST-G), 106–107
Shultz, K. S., 1, 14, 16, 22, 26, 27,
　　58, 79
Simoni-Wastila, L., 86, 88, 89, 90, 91,
　　92, 93, 99
Skinner, H. A., 63, 95
sleep-related problems, 78–79
　alcohol misuse to manage, 79–83, 131
　gender as boundary condition, 80
　insomnia, 81, *90*, 130, 131
　opioids and benzodiazepines for, 91
　Pittsburgh Sleep Quality Index,
　　82–83
　secondary effect of stress, 80
　as source of anxiety, 80
　tranquilizers or sleeping pills for, 81
Sloan, F. A., 8, 12, 13, 23, *37*, 39, 40, 42,
　　44, 46, 61, 127
Smithers Institute for Alcohol-Related
　　Workplace Studies (Cornell
　　University), 17–18, 123
Smothers, B., 11
social bonds, 25
social control theory, 25–26
　model, 31, *31*
social interaction
　alcohol use and, 21
　work-based, 3
socialization, 25
social learning, 25
social media, 116

social networks
　auto workers compared, 120–121
　postretirement challenges, 70
　workplace social networks, 60–62, 68
social networks theory, 22–24
　model, 30–31, *31*
　new, and alcohol use, 25
　social isolation and, 29
social norming, 104
social resources, assessing, 72
Social Security Act (1935), 132
social selection, among heavy drinkers,
　　75
social support networks, 23–24
　AA peer-based support, 108–109
　measuring support, 60–61
　retiree drinking problems related, 62
Soghikian, K., 44
Sonnenstuhl, W., 40, 47, 60, 65, 67, 85,
　　93, 96, 97, 111, 127
specificity of screening tools, 103
Stacy, A. W., 64, 65, 66
Stanford Study, 71–78
status inconsistency, 125–126
stress. *See also* coping with stress
　alcohol misuse related, 21
　bridge employment, 16–17
　coping style and alcohol misuse, 13
　as drain on psychological resources, 80
　drug abuse and early retirement, 98
　early-middle stage of retirement
　　adjustment, 70–71
　early retirement, 98
　financial, 47, 49
　impact on other variables, 84
　leaving stressful environment as pro-
　　tective factor, 68
　patterns of alcohol use and, 27
　potential new stressors, 21
　sleep-related problems, 78–79, 80–83
　status inconsistency, 125–126
　stress climate and drinking norms,
　　63–64, 123
　transition timing and, 27
　unit-level stress climate, 62–64
　workplace stress and gender, 55–57
stress and coping perspective, 20–21
　evaluated, 20
　moderated medial model based
　　on, 29